Nathan,
Enjoy the

Stephen Mulligan

Were You There?

Over 300 Wonderful, Weird, and Wacky Moments from the Pittsburgh Civic/Mellon Arena

by

Stephen Mulligan

RoseDog🐾Books

PITTSBURGH, PENNSYLVANIA 15222

The contents of this work including, but not limited to, the accuracy of events, people, and places depicted; opinions expressed; permission to use previously published materials included; and any advice given or actions advocated are solely the responsibility of the author, who assumes all liability for said work and indemnifies the publisher against any claims stemming from publication of the work.

All Rights Reserved
Copyright © 2011 by Stephen Mulligan

No part of this book may be reproduced or transmitted, downloaded, distributed, reverse engineered, or stored in or introduced into any information storage and retrieval system, in any form or by any means, including photocopying and recording, whether electronic or mechanical, now known or hereinafter invented without permission in writing from the publisher.

RoseDog Books
701 Smithfield Street
Pittsburgh, PA 15222
Visit our website at *www.rosedogbookstore.com*

ISBN: 978-1-4349-8552-1
eISBN: 978-1-4349-7547-8

Introduction

The Pittsburgh Mellon Arena (formerly the Civic Arena/Auditorium) has hosted thousands of events in its history. From its opening on September 17, 1961 to its final day June 26, 2010 it played a vital role in the development of Pittsburgh's sporting and cultural life. Designed originally as a multi-purpose facility and the new home of the Pittsburgh Civic Light Opera the "Igloo" as many locals have called it welcomed five decades worth of splendid activities sprinkled with the occasional off-side. This once architectural wonder with its state of the art retractable roof represented all that Pittsburgh was- strong at the core (steel) but with an open eye (retractable roof) to the future!

Now that the granddaddy of arenas has reached the end of its "goal" let's not feel sad but rather celebrate some of its greatest moments. In this book I have highlighted over 300 **"Were you there?"** moments at the Pittsburgh Civic/Mellon Arena. Included is at least one event from each year of its existence. Most of these events herein described have a positive tinge. Some however are "lowlights" yet nonetheless important when detailing the sum of the whole. Another criterion that I have looked at in describing these events has been variety. As most folks know, the Pittsburgh Penguins have been the main tenants of the Civic/Mellon Arena since 1967 and have certainly provided a boat load of highs and lows. However there has been a host of other sporting, cultural and religious events that have provided "spills and chills" for all in attendance. I have tried to showcase these and others that may be considered even strange or bizarre. Have there been more than 300 **"Were you there?"** moments. Certainly! Each event that you have attended or participated in at the Pittsburgh Mellon/Civic Arena could have been your **"Were you there?"** moment.

Chapter 1, 1961-1965

1961

1) September 17

The new kid is christened

Were you there for the Opening Ceremonies of the spanking brand new Pittsburgh Civic Auditorium/Arena? If so, you were among 5,000 people who witnessed a piece of Pittsburgh and world history. After years of planning and three and a half years of construction, the "Dome" was ready for its coming out party. Folks first gathered outside the new auditorium where Mayor Joseph Barr, the governor, and other dignitaries cut the ceremonial ribbon. After some short speeches and music by Joe Morrone's band, the delighted crowd moved indoors with much anticipation. Upon entering many marveled at the size and architectural design of the place. Pride and wonder filled the air. Soon Conductor Karl Kritz of the Pittsburgh Symphony and his 50-piece orchestra performed Star-Spangled Banner as their first number. After some more short speeches the crowd got another treat. High above their heads, two sections of the state-of-the-art retractable roof started to move. Two and a half minutes later the audience awed at the opening sky view. The sun shined on them and the city of Pittsburgh. What a great day for the city! One of the dignitaries present that day was Spanish Ambassador Mariano deYturralde. Upon hearing the beautiful music and seeing the roof "disappear" he told the mayor "It's the eighth wonder of the world".

2) September 18-30

A dazzling debut

The Ice Capades became the first shows of any kind to perform at the new Civic Arena. For 13 days, ice dancers of all kind delighted curious onlookers. Everyone wanted to see what all the fuss was about. Superstar skaters Sonja Heine and Dick Button led the charge with multiple jumps and twists. Meanwhile, 27 chorus-style skaters called the "Ice Ca pets" and the Ice Cadets danced in unison to various musical numbers. These included: A salute to Lerner and Loewe, My Fair Lady, Camelot, Disneyrama and many others.

During one specific performance on September 19[th,] (only the 3rd day since the Civic Arena was opened) audience members got to see skaters under the open roof. Everything was going fine until the weather changed. Just 22 minutes into the show, outside temperatures reached a balmy 74 degrees and there was fear the ice would start to melt. Thanks to the quick action of arena staff the dome was closed and the show continued without a hitch.

Did you know Dick Button won 2 Olympic gold medals-one in 1948 and the other in1952? Sonja Heine did one better winning Olympic gold medals in 1928, 1932 and 1936.

3) October 3-12

This place feels like home!

For ten days the Civic Arena held the biggest Home Show to date in Pittsburgh. One unique aspect of this event was the Mrs. America contest. The contest was open to women at least 21 years old and married. Judges were looking for homemaking skills and other factors like; poise, personality, grooming and participation in community affairs. The winner would be named Mrs. Pennsylvania and would later compete against other state winners in Fort Lauderdale, Florida.

Did you know the eventual winner of the Mrs. America contest was Mrs. Michigan? Her name was Mrs. Lila Masson and she lived in Detroit.

4) October 14

Let the games begin!

Were you there to see the Buffalo Bisons of the American Hockey League (AHL) defeat the Pittsburgh Hornets 2-1 in the first hockey game ever played at the Civic Arena? In front of a crowd of 9,317 hungry fans (about 3/4 capacity) twenty-one year old Hornet defenseman Paul Jackson (St. Michael College Majors) would get the honor of scoring the team's first goal. Ironically for Jackson, this would be his only goal of the season! Also playing for the Hornets that year would be future Boston Bruin star goalie Gerry Cheevers.

The Hornets were the AHL affiliates of the Detroit Red Wings of the National Hockey League (NHL). They originally started playing in1936 and were Calder Cup Champions in 1952 and 1955. In 1956 the team folded when the Duquesne Gardens was torn down. The new Hornets would re-emerge in1961 and played 6 years at the Civic Arena. In the spring of 1967 they won their third and last Calder Cup. In same year, as the Pittsburgh Penguins made their debut in the NHL, the Hornets folded.

Did you know the Pittsburgh Hornets (1966-67) and the Buffalo Bisons (1969-70) won Calder Cups in their last year of existence? In the following years both cities received NHL franchises.

5) October 17

They were bouncing off the ropes!

A month after the opening of the Civic Arena, 8,442 pumped up fans came to the first ever wrestling show. Throughout the night, 20 big sweaty men pounded on each other in 10 separate matches. Many of the performing wrestlers would become regulars to the Civic Arena and household names in Pittsburgh. Up until 1976, the Steel Belt Wrestling circuit produced some memorable characters not the least of which was local champ and favorite Bruno Sammartino.

For those curious about the outcome of the 10 matches, the results were: 1) Buddy Rogers defeated Johnny Valentine 2/3 falls, 2) Crusher Lisowski defeated Haystacks Calhoun, 3) The Fabulous Kangaroos defeated Antonio Rocca and Argentina Apollo, 4) Ace Freeman and Zivko Kovacic defeated Ronnie and Ronnie Fargo, 5) Sailor Art Thomas defeated Fred Atkins, 6) Bruno Sammartino defeated Tommy O'Toole, 7) Alexander Kostopoulos defeated Skull Murphy, 8) Eddie Faietta defeated Angelo Savoldi, 9) Mike Paidousis defeated Jack Terry and 10) Mickey Sharp drew Billy Fox.

6) October 19

The "Wizard of Oz" star comes to the Steel City

On this night Judy Garland became the first artist of any kind to perform a concert at the spanking brand new Pittsburgh Civic Arena. Depending on what sources you read it was either the best or worst show ever. For true fans of the movie and music legend it was a beautiful performance in a beautiful new building. They were captivated by Garland's every move as she blew kisses and sang hit after hit including: For Me and My Gal, Come Rain or Come Shine, Stormy Weather and Over the Rainbow. For others who may have been just curious on-lookers, the show, which started late, had both sound and lighting problem throughout. Despite the differences in opinion, the audience that night got to witness an unprecedented 6 encores-the last 2 of which with the houselights on. The attendance of 12,219 was the first sell-out at the arena. Were you there?

Did you know one of the musicians for the Judy Garland concert was local bass player Emil Brenkus?

7) October 20

I found my thrill on Blueberry Hill (District)

One day after the Judy Garland concert, the Civic Arena continued the music with its first ever multi-act performance. The name, Rock and Roll Show included appearances by: Fats Domino, 16 year-old Brenda Lee-"Little Miss Dynamite", Jay T. Reid, The Casuals, Bob Beckham and The La Rells. As it turns out the La Rells would be the first Pittsburgh vocal group to appear at the "Igloo". Disc Jockey Clark Race (KDKA, Pittsburgh), served as Master of Ceremonies while instrumental background was provided by the Gi Gi Greene Orchestra.

The billing of multiple artists on the same night would be a common occurrence at the Civic Arena. Throughout the 1960's various radio stations sponsored and co-hosted these events.

Did you know who picked up Brenda Lee at the airport upon her arrival in Pittsburgh? It was the La Rells. Lee was with her mother and they joined the La Rells for lunch thereafter.

8) November 7

Two hoops in a package…

With a sold-out crowd on their side, the Pittsburgh Renaissance (Rens) basketball team slam-dunked the Chicago Majors 105-90. This was the Rens second home game of the season and fans lapped it up. As inaugural members of the American Basketball League (ABL), Pittsburgh boasted 19-year-old rookie sensation Connie Hawkins. On this particular night the youngster led all shooters with 27 points. His scoring exploits in this game and those that would follow garnered him the league M.V.P. for 1961-62. Hawkins would soon become a future star in the ABA and later in the NBA.

The Rens were the first professional basketball team to play at the Pittsburgh Civic Arena. In their inaugural season they would record 41 wins and 40 losses. In their second year the team started with a respectable 12 wins and 10 losses but then bad news happened. On December 31, 1962 the whole league disbanded!

The 13,816 fans attending the above game were also there for another reason. A preliminary game featuring the world famous Harlem Globetrotters was played. Fans all around Pittsburgh wanted to see the fancy tricks and spins that these court artists employed. After all, this was the most popular basketball team in the world! Records of this special night show 1000 or more fans not counted in the attendance figures. Why was this? Anxious to get in they broke through unguarded gates at the Civic Arena. Meanwhile an estimated 5,000 more were turned away at the doors.

By the way, the Globetrotters won the game that night beating their long time rivals the Washington Generals 67 to 57.

Did you know the Harlem Globetrotter game played on November 7, 1961 was their 7,500[th] in their 35-year history?

9) November 21-25

Trapeze Trouble

The famous Ringling Brothers and Barnum and Bailey Circus performed at the Civic Arena for 5 days. Bright eyed kids from all over the region were delighted by the unique and unusual performances. Many were awed by the animals especially the 17 pok-a-dot elephants that would be part of the entertainment. However not all was fun and games. On the night of November 23rd an unfortunate incident occurred in the air of the Civic Arena. A 27-year old trapeze artist named Maria Dos Santos fell ten feet from a rope and crashed to the ground. The audience was in shock as they witnessed the terrible fall. Soon help was on the way. Meanwhile the stunned crowd wondered if Dos Santos was going to be all right. An ambulance team was on the scene and transported her to the Mercy Hospital. A short time later Dos Santos received x-rays to her right elbow and shoulder. She was definitely injured but the prognosis was good. Eventually Dos Santos fully recovered. When asked later about the accident, she said it happened as a result of a fainting spell.

10) December 6

Basketball came with a taste of baseball, football and boxing.

Were you there to see this basket ball triple-header? In the first tilt, local universities Duquesne and Carnegie Tech took to the hardwood. The powerful Dukes came out flying and scored almost at will. They kept the pressure on all night as they cruised to a 78 to 40 victory.

The second game was a fun exhibition one between Pittsburgh Pirates players and their alumni. One Pirate-Dick Groat was no stranger to the sport as he had played pro basketball in the NBA. Even the referees that night had some notoriety. They were then current Pittsburgh Steeler players Bobby Layne and Gene "Big Daddy" Liscomb. Sporting fans got a special bonus as former middleweight and welterweight boxing champion Sugar Ray Robinson was an audience guest. He was in town for an upcoming match (more to come on this…).

The final game of the night and the one the crowd of 7,221 was waiting for saw mighty Ohio State take on the Pittsburgh Panthers. At the time Ohio was the defending NCAA national champions. Their team boasted three All-Americans in the likes of John Havlicek, Jerry Lucas (both who went on to have great NBA careers) and Bobby Knight (coach with the most wins in college history). The game was exciting as both team made some terrific shots. Unfortunately for the pro-Pittsburgh fans Ohio's superior play and talent rose to the top as they coasted to a 99 to 79 win.

11) December 8

The sweet science makes its debut

This was the date of the first boxing match at the Pittsburgh Civic Arena. It featured former welterweight and middleweight champ "Sugar" Ray Robinson against former Canadian Commonwealth champ (1954) Wilf

Greaves. Both boxers had met in Detroit 2 and 1/2 months before with Robinson squeaking out a 10-round decision. In that fight Robinson did go down in the 8th round but was able to recover. At the time of this fight in Pittsburgh, Greaves had just turned 26 (the day before) while Robinson was much older at 40. Each fighter tipped the scales at 161.5 pounds.

The first round started cautiously with the boxers feeling each other out. In the second round Greaves put Robinson down but couldn't finish him. Robinson rebounded and got through the round. The next five rounds were pretty even with each getting some good pokes in. As the 8th round started Robinson seemed to have some extra energy. He caught Greaves with a series of punches that put him down. Greaves couldn't get up for the standing count. It was over at the 43 seconds mark-Robinson won his 146th match by knockout!

Did you know that "Sugar" Ray Robinson became the welterweight champion in 1946 and then held the title for the next 5 years?

12) December 16

The 'City Game' finds a new home

The annual City Game between the Pittsburgh Panthers men's basketball team and the Duquesne Dukes made its debut at the Civic Arena. The teams met in the final of the Steel Bowl Tournament. On this day in front of a crowd of 6,452 Duquesne beat Pittsburgh 73 to 70. Willie Somerset led the Dukes with 25 points.

Duquesne earned the right to be in the final when they upset Duke 66 to 61 in the first round.

Did you know the first City Game was played on January 13, 1932 at the Pitt Pavilion? Duquesne also won that game 28 to 21. However, as of 2008 Pittsburgh has a better record with 46 wins and 31 losses.

1962

13) January 6

Only one player to start a hockey game

On this bizarre night, the Buffalo Bisons hockey team beat the Pittsburgh Hornets twice in one evening. This was certainly one of the strangest sporting events ever at the Civic Arena. Why was there 2 games played that evening? Well it started back a month earlier (December 6, 1961) when these same two teams met before. In that game, while leading 4-2, the Bisons were awarded a penalty shot with 9:50 left in the third period. Had they scored Buffalo would have built a comfortable 3-goal lead. However, the Pittsburgh goalie stopped the shot with a brilliant save. Then as regular play continued, neither team would score another goal and Buffalo preserved the 4-2 victory. At the end of the game, the Hornets were angry and protested. They claimed the wrong player was awarded the penalty shot. Upon later review, AHL officials agreed with Pittsburgh. The league then declared the third period would restart at 9:50 with the "right" player taking the penalty shot as the two teams met again on January 6. Well the shortened third period did start as prescribed and again the Hornet goalie stopped the puck. As regular play resumed Pittsburgh managed to score another goal before the end of the game but still lost the contest 4 to 3. In the complete game that followed, the Hornets continued their bad luck and lost 3-0.

14) January 15

A good effort wasted

In basketball action the Cleveland Pipers squeaked by the Pittsburgh Rens 110-108. What was strange about this close scoring game was the dominance of Rens star Connie Hawkins. He pumped in 54 points-exactly half of the teams output! It was sad the home team lost but there was some consolation in defeat. Hawkins broke the ABL record for most points in a game. The previous mark of 51 was held by Roger Kaiser of the New York Tapers.

Did you know on this same day there was another ABL game played at the Civic Arena? In that one, the Kansas City Steers defeated the New York Tapers 122-96.

15) February 21

How many boxers does it take…?

The 17th Annual Post-Gazette Dapper Dan Golden Gloves punched its way into the Civic Arena. On this mid-winter night, 8,478 pump-up spectators witnessed a marathon of boxing. In fact fifty-four boxers got a chance to show off their stuff. A total of 27 bouts in 3 categories were contested. While some heavy weights came in over 200 pounds, others at the opposite end tipped the scales at a buck twelve.

One of the highlights of the evening came in the 139-pound junior novice class. It featured Teddy Chernoff against Donald Christopher. In the first round Christopher hit Chernoff hard and put him off balance. Chernoff shook off the pain and pursued his opponent. He caught him and hit Christopher with a flurry of shots that floored him. Christopher managed to get up but Chernoff sensing victory, whacked him again with a south paw hook. This was all she wrote. Christopher tried to get up for the second round but referee Tarzan McGivern stopped the fight. Chernoff was declared the winner by TKO. This, as it turns out was his 4th straight one-round victory. For his efforts that night Chernoff received the outstanding boxing trophy.

Did you know this was the first time the Golden Gloves were held at the Civic Arena?

16) March 29

Wow! Two extra periods played in one day.

This was a special evening because 4 ABL basketball teams played in 2 separate play-off games. Both were one shot affairs with winners moving on to the next round. Ironically the ABL also had first-half season play-offs with Kansas City emerging the winner.

Meanwhile back at the Civic Arena the paltry crowd of 3,453 settled in for the double header. In the first game the Washington/N.Y.Tapers took on the Hawaii Chiefs. Both teams fought hard all game. By the end of regulation play the score was tied. In overtime, led by the brilliant play of Dan Swartz the Tapers emerged with a 125 to 116 victory. Swartz would lead all players that day with 42 points.

After a close first game, fans were anxious to see their Pittsburgh Rens in the next one. Their opponents would be the San Francisco Saints. However, before the ball toss some business was attended to. Pittsburgh Mayor Joseph M. Barr honored Rens superstar Connie Hawkins with the league MVP plague, an automobile and other minor gifts. The audience applauded in appreciation.

The game soon got under way and both teams came out flying. Like the previous contest both teams seemed evenly matched. Hawkins got his usual buckets but the Rens couldn't sustain any momentum. The lead kept going back and forth. The second half was no different and the score reflected it. When the final buzzer sounded it was even Steven. Again overtime would be needed to determine a winner. In the extra frame, the Rens couldn't pull it out and fell just short losing 107 to 103. Hawkins' 41 points weren't enough on this day.

Did you know who the eventual second-half league champs were? They were the Cleveland Pipers who by the way were owned by a group of investors headed by a young George Steinbrenner.

17) April 22

No miracle in the sky this day!

Over 10,000 worshipers flocked to the Civic Arena for an Easter Sunrise Service. Some of the faithful must have had sleep in their eyes considering things got started at 6:30am! Many were expecting to see the roof open since temperatures that day were expected to reach 80 degrees. However disappointed filled the air when Reverend Dr. Harold R. Albert, president of the Council of Churches of the Pittsburgh Area and pastor of the First Lutheran Church made an announcement. He said the dome couldn't be open because the weather sealing agent used on the dome during the winter had not been removed. What a downer!

Did you know this was the 32nd annual Easter Sunrise Service but the first one held at the Civic Arena?

18) May 1-5

A bundle of joy arrives

The Syria Shrine Circus 'delivers' something special. Though this wasn't the first circus act at the Civic Arena something unusual did happen on the evening of May 2nd. At 8:25pm just as the Master of Ceremonies James Allen blew the whistle to open the show, a Mrs. Mary Clothier gave birth to an 8-pound 3-ounce baby girl. Mrs. Clothier and her husband who was a circus vendor had been staying in a trailer that was parked in the garage inside the Civic Arena. Needless to say this was a pleasant surprise for the family and historical because it was the first baby ever born at the Civic Arena.

Did you know this was the Clothiers' fifth child and the second one not born in a hospital? The families' fourth child was born in a car while father Albert was rushing Mary through Detroit traffic to a hospital.

19) May 11

The Igloo gets hit hard

The Porky Chedwick Groove Spectacular is presented at the Civic Arena. This night boasted a boat load of performers that included: Jackie Wilson, Bo Diddley, The Flamingos, The Marvellettes, The Five Satins, Jerry Butler, Ketty Lester, Johnny Jack, The Skyliners (Pittsburgh), Patti LaBelle and the BlueBelles, The Castells, Bobby Vinton (Canonsburg), The Drifters, The Debonaires, Gene Pitney, The Coasters, The Angels, The Jive Five, The Carousels, Big Maybelle, The Shirells and Hank Ballard. This was perhaps the biggest multi-billed show that Pittsburgh has ever seen. While more than 13,000 fans enjoyed the show inside it was a different story outside. More than 3,000 people who couldn't get tickets to the sold-out show started throwing rocks and bottles at the Civic Arena dome!

Did you know that the Skyliners were the first Pittsburgh musical group to play at the Civic Arena? By the way, they still play now. Did you also know Bo Diddley's sidekick was Pittsburgh native Norma Jean Wofford (a.k.a.'The Duchess').

20) June 3

An academic affair

Were you there when the Civic Arena hosted its first ever graduation ceremony? Almost 800 lucky students from Duquesne University received their degrees this day. They would become the first of a long list of students in the Pittsburgh area to have their commencements held at the Igloo. Dr. Charles Malik, philosopher, historian and professor at American University, Washington D.C. gave the commencement address while also receiving an honorary doctor of humanities degree. Dr. Helen White and Richard Wright also received honorary degrees that day.

Did you know Kathryn Jean Figler, a Math Major at Duquesne was the only student in1962 that graduated *summa cum laude* (with highest honors)?

21) July 2-7

A funny lady comes to town

The Carol Burnett Review teamed up with the Pittsburgh Civic Light Opera (CLO) for 6 nights of comedy and fun. These shows were historical as the

CLO made their Civic Arena debut. However, more importantly and lesser known was the fact the Civic Arena was initially designed and built for the CLO. It was to become their permanent home and a showcase to the entertainment world. Unfortunately, due to specific structural nuances that caused production problems, the CLO would soon abandon the Civic Arena for greener pastures.

Despite issues with the building the CLO did bring some big names to Pittsburgh. Carol Burnett, for example, who was already a television star at the time, drew a large following. With her unique delivery style and variety of songs, jokes and imitations, she kept audience members laughing all night. On her July 4th performance, when the retractable dome was opened for the first time ever for an evening performance Burnett quipped "Ladies and Gentlemen, allow me to present…The Sky." In the 6 days she was in town 42,121 customers came to see her.

A big part of The Carol Burnett Revue featured the comedy team of Pittsburgh's Marty Allen and New York's Steve Rossi. Ken Welch who wrote the show was a graduate of Carnegie Tech. and the Pittsburgh Playhouse.

Did you know Carol Burnett who was 29 years old at the time was divorced in September, 1962 from husband actor Don Saroyan?

22) July 10-15

The nutty professor is in the house

Soon after a funny lady (Carol Burnett) delighted Civic Arena audiences a funny man followed. The Jerry Lewis Revue came to town for another 6-day gig. This was the second performance the Pittsburgh Civic Opera ever presented at the Civic Arena. Not a bad 1-2 punch. The 36-year old Lewis, like Burnett was no stranger to the viewing public. In previous years he had hooked up with Dean Martin to form the famous Martin and Lewis comedy team. Not only did they entertain live, but starred in many comical films in their ten-year pairing.

His show at the Civic Arena continued with his wacky sense of comedy. He did skits, imitations and jokes to the approval of his audience. If you were there you may recall a special feature with singer/actor Della Reese as "the Queen of Wails". Other performers included: "The Rocky-Fellers", The Los Gatos, The Modernaires, and Peg Leg Bates.

Did you know when Jerry Lewis arrived in Pittsburgh he had 64 pieces of baggage, an entourage of 7, 25 dinner jackets and a set of golf clubs which he tested at Oakmont?

23) August 7-12

A young star shines through

Switching gears from the review-type shows, the Civic Light Opera continued their 1962 summer program with 'Gypsy.' This was one of the first musical productions Civic Arena audiences got to see and featured veteran performer and singer extraordinaire Betty Hutton. Her resume included: The Miracle of Morgan's Creek (1944), Annie Get Your Gun (1950) and The Greatest Show on Earth (1952). In 'Gypsy' she would perform Mama Rose and did an admirable job. For many though, another rising star captured their hearts this day. It was the performance the young 14 year-old Bernadette Peters in her role as Dainty June that blew them away. For such a small girl, her voice was clear and powerful.

Did you know Betty Hutton passed away on March 12, 2007? She was 86 years old.

24) August 14-19

This one is money in the bank

Riding the musical theme, "Oklahoma" rode into town. It starred Robert Horton (from the television show "Wagon Train") as Curly, Hal LeRoy (Show Boat), Jack DeLon (Livin' The Life), Laurie Franks (Around the World in 80 Days) and Betty Gillette as Ado Annie in her Civic Light Opera debut. Gillette would go on to perform over 70 stage productions in her illustrious career including many in Pittsburgh. Her performance in 'Oklahoma' along with her companions made the CLO more money than any other musical presented that summer.

25) August 27-September 1

Belafonte gets a new name

To cap off a nice summer run, Harry Belafonte performed with the Pittsburgh Civic Light Opera. The man with the smooth and silky voice delighted the audience with an array of folk and calypso favorites that included: Matilda,

Mule Skinner Blues, Betty and Dupree and John Henry. Special guest for these performances was African songstress Mariam Makeba. She sang in native tongues including: Congo, Xosa and Zulu. She also did her famous "Boot Dance" and teamed up with Belafonte for Man Smart.

Did you know Belafonte inherited a new first name when he was performing in Pittsburgh? Yes, an employee of the Penn-Sheraton Hotel had put up a sign on the marquee of the Grant Street entrance which read **Barry** Belafonte.

1963

26) January 14

The greatest "Wingman" comes to the Burgh

On this hockey night in Pittsburgh, the AHL Pittsburgh Hornets whipped the NHL Detroit Red Wings 7-4 in an exhibition game. Over 8,000 curious fans came out to the Civic Arena to see "Mr. Hockey" Gordie Howe and his teammates play in a charity fundraiser for the Children's Hospital. The game itself was a close scoring affair for 2 periods. Then in the third, Hornets Warren Hynes scored 3 goals in less than 5 minutes to blow it wide open.

For those wondering how Howe performed that night, he scored 1 goal while teammates Norm Ullman and Alex Dellvecchio had 2 and 1 respectively.

Howe, who was the perennial leader of the Red Wings, would go on to have an excellent 1962-63 NHL campaign. That year he captured the Art Ross Memorial trophy for winning the scoring race (38 goals and 48 assists for 86 points) and added the Hart Memorial trophy for being the most valuable player to his team. His Red Wings also went to the Stanley Cup Finals but lost to the Toronto Maple Leafs in 5 games.

Did you know the Pittsburgh Hornets who were the American Hockey League affiliates of the Detroit Red Wings played each other 10 times in exhibition games from 1962 to 1965?

27) January 19

An Olympic size beating

Soon after the Red Wings left town, the Civic Arena hosted another distinguished hockey team. This time it was the U.S. Olympic Team who, not only were talented but were the defending gold medal winners (1960 Winter

Olympics in Squaw Valley, California). Their challengers would be the Pittsburgh Knights, an amateur hockey team from the Mid-Atlantic Hockey League.

It didn't take very long to see who the superior team was. Team U.S. scored early and often while peppering 71 shots at the Knights goalie Rudy Domitrovic and later Pete Burchfield. By the end of the night, the Knights were demolished 17-1. Team U.S was led by Jerry Westby and Marschall Tschida who both had 3 goals each (hat tricks). Bill Downey had the lone goal for Pittsburgh in the second period. Ironically, it was the Knights first defeat all season.

Did you know a couple months after this game the U.S. Olympic Team played in the World Hockey Championships in Sweden? This time they would be the big losers finishing last among 8 countries.

28) January 24

Clay makes good on a promise

The day started out cold and remained that way. Schools were closed, a snow blizzard blanketed Pittsburgh and temperatures dipped well below 0. Despite the miserable day 21-year old Cassius Clay (later called Mohammed Ali) was in town and he was going to box at the Civic Arena. Nicknamed the "Louisville Lip", Clay was in his usual talkative mood before the fight. He predicted he would win in three rounds. His opponent Charley Powell was bigger and more muscular and was not intimidated by him. Powell approached the fight with the philosophy that he would take a couple punches in order to give a few punches. The philosophy worked well for the first couple rounds. However, Clay's deceptive punches soon took their toll. Then Clay "floated like a butterfly and stung like a bee" and knocked Charley Powell out in round three (at 2:04 to be exact). Just as predicted, Clay had won his bout and was well on his way to becoming the world champ.

The 11,238 fans that came to the Civic Arena that night not only saw the self proclaimed "greatest boxer of all time" but made some local history also. They broke an attendance record for a pro fight in Pittsburgh. The event could have been sold out (13,000) but many stayed home because of the inclement weather.

Did you know Charley Powell was an ex-professional football player? He had played for the San Francisco 49'ers and the Oakland Raiders.

29) March 12

"Big John" has a big "Knight"

In one of the classic matches in the Western Pennsylvania Interscholastic Athletic League (WPIAL), the Norwin Knights high school basketball team took on the Aliquippa Quips in the class A final. The Knights, led by "Big John" Naponick were looking to upset the talented Quips.

The game (the first high school one ever played at the Civic Arena) started evenly and stood that way for almost 4 periods. In fact, 5 times during the seesaw battle the score was tied. Sixteen–year old Naponick, who stood 6'8" and weighed 285, took his share of pounding underneath the net but continued to make baskets for the Knights. In fact he scored almost half his teams' points with 33 as Norwin pulled out a 69-64 victory. The win gave Norwin their first school title.

Did you know 10,718 people showed up for this game? This was only the second sell-out in Civic Arena history. The first one was on October 19, 1961 when Judy Garland came to town.

30) October 3

Hometown singer puts it on television

Were you there when 51 year-old Perry Como taped his NBC TV Spectacular show at the Civic Arena? Como who hailed from Canonsburg, Pennsylvania (just 20 miles south of Pittsburgh) returned "home" to produce his first television special. Previously, the former barber-turned-singer enjoyed a 15-year run on weekly radio and television shows that concluded with "the Kraft Music Hall" on June 12, 1963. The popular "Mr. C" had such hits as: Prisoner of Love, Don't Let the Stars Get in Your Eyes, Hot Diggity, Catch a Falling Star and Papa Loves Mambo.

On this night back at the Civic Arena, Como had special guests including: film and television actress June Allyson, comedian/actor George Burns, dancer/actress Cyd Charisse, actor/dancer James Mitchell, writer /producer /parodist Allan Sherman and the Mitchell Ayers Orchestra.

If you remember your television programs, Sherman was the original voice of the Cat in the Hat. Mitchell meanwhile played Palmer Cortlandt on All My Children for 30 years until his death in 2010. The Mitchell Ayers Orchestra had been with Perry Como for 15 years including "The Chesterfield Supper Club."

Did you know Perry Como died on May 12, 2001? He was just 6 days short of his 89ᵗʰ birthday.

31) December 20

What? No knock-outs all night?

In one of the shortest boxing matches at the Civic Arena, Rubin "Hurricane" Carter (No.2 Middle Weight Contender) made short work of World Welterweight Champion Emile Griffith. Fans barely got seated for this main event when the "Hurricane" unleashed on Griffith. Griffith was so stunned the ref called for a standing 9-count. Shortly after, the barrage continued. Griffith was in trouble again and this time the ref called it off. Carter had won by TKO at just 2:13 of the first round. This was certainly not a good night for the Champ!

At least the 5,436 people who did show up saw some preliminary fights. The results were: Cowboy Billy Smith won a split decision over fellow Ohioan Tommy Fix, Canadian Fernand "The Bull" Chretien beat Calvin Woodland in a TKO, Bernard Forbes took care of Jimmy Levers in a fourth round TKO, Don "Toro" Smith (Homewood) got by Vic Brown in a technically stopped match while Carl "Baby" Baldwin (Toronto) disposed of Billy Wagner. Throughout the evening, no knock-outs occurred.

1964

32) April 5

The post-season is finally a reality

Were you there to see the Quebec Aces play the Pittsburgh Hornets in the first ever American Hockey League (AHL) playoff game at the Civic Arena? Both teams had entered the post-season having finished atop their respective divisions. Furthermore, each had accumulated 83 points.

The crowd of 9,187 (3/4 capacity) witnessed a pretty tight game accept for a couple of glaring defensive lapses for the Hornets. The result would produce not 1 but 2 breakaway goals for the Aces. Some other minor miscues from Pittsburgh gave Quebec 2 more goals that eventually put the game out of reach. The final score was 4-1 for the visitors from the Great White North.

Unfortunately for the Hornets, not only would they lose the game but eventually the playoff series 4 games to 1. As for Quebec they had a couple aces up their sleeves in the likes of NHL experienced goalie Lorne "Gump" Worsley and the former legendary defenseman from the Montreal Canadiens Doug Harvey. Their team made it to the Calder Cup finals this year before bowing out to the Cleveland Barons 4 games to 0.

Did you know the Quebec Aces had never made the AHL playoffs until this year?

33) June 5

Glad All Over

On this night The Dave Clark Five band stormed the Civic Arena with gusto. As part of the British music invasion to the U.S., the five lads from London/Tottenham had fans hot and bothered. Their show was great but was interrupted 3 times as obsessed teenagers jumped on the stage. The police, trying to restore peace, ordered the rabid crowd off each time. However, the pandemonium continued and finally the concert had to be shortened. There were just too many screaming girls that were causing havoc.

One reason why the 6,000 fans were so pumped up and noisy may be traced backed to the week before. This is when The Dave Clark Five made an appearance on the Ed Sullivan Show.

If you were at this show you may recall the opening act. They were an all-female group from Cleveland called The Secrets. Does their song "The Boy Next Door" ring a bell?

Did you know after their concert the Dave Clark Five still couldn't get any peace and quiet? It was reported that 3,000 fans jammed the lobby of their hotel (Carlton House) to get another look at them. Again police had to be called over to disperse the crowd.

34) June 20-23

A great President is remembered

Seven months after President John F. Kennedy was assassinated a Traveling Exhibit of his personal possessions came to the Civic Arena. This assortment of artifacts, tastefully displayed, included: papers, mementos, doodling, a rocking chair and his desk from the White House. Items in the collection came from JFK's life as a boy, congressman, senator and President. The final destination for the various papers and mementos was to be the JFK Library which was going to be built on the banks of the Charles River in Boston.

On one particular day of the JFK Exhibit in Pittsburgh (June21) things got a bit sticky. It started early as crowds gathered outside the Civic Arena 2 hours before the doors opened. Meanwhile temperatures were steadily climbing to a blistering 90 degrees. Officials at the Arena gave people a break by letting them in early. This was a temporary relief but soon other problems came up. First, the size of the crowd throughout the day reached 12,000 and second, the lineups for the most popular displays kept getting bigger and bigger. The result was some folks; especially the real old and the real young, succumbed to the heat. By the end of the day it was reported 5 adults and 3 children had fainted!

Did you know the day before the JFK Exhibit opened in Pittsburgh; the late Senator Edward Kennedy (the 32-year old younger brother of JFK) was seriously injured in a private plane crash in Southampton, Massachusetts? The accident claimed 2 lives while 2 others were injured.

35) August 10-15

A classic performer shows her talent

The Pittsburgh Civic Light Opera's production of Tovarich was presented at the Civic Arena on these six days. This musical/comedy featured half of one of the greatest dancing teams ever-Ginger Rogers. From 1933-1939 Rogers paired with Fred Astaire to revolutionize the Hollywood musical. Fast forward to 1964, the 53 year-old Rogers looked 35 and sang and danced like it to. The highlight of the evenings came when she did a number called "Wilkes Barre, P.A.". She performed it chorus-girl style as she exited the stage, then re-entered doing the Charleston, then exited, re-entered, exited and re-entered again.

While Ginger Rogers was in Pittsburgh her driver for the week was David Newell. You might remember him as Mr. "McFeely" on Mr. Rogers' Neighborhood.

Did you know Ginger Rogers made 73 movies in her career? Ten of these were musical ones with her partner Fred Astaire.

36) September 14

The British Invasion continues!

The Beatles take the "Burgh" by storm. There was so much buzz leading up to this concert that the City of Pittsburgh had to hire extra security to deal with the hoopla. It all started early on the morning of September 14 as 120 county police and deputy sheriffs (including for the first time 15 Allegheny County Mounted Police) merged at the Pittsburgh Airport. Some fans were there at 9am though the "Mop Tops" were only expected at 4pm from Baltimore. After many hours of waiting and the arrival time nearing, the crowd swelled to 4,000. Each plane landing was met with yells and screams. Finally around 4:40pm the boys landed and the crowd went berserk. Some fans got a quick glimpse of their favorite band members but security was tight. Soon after, the Beatles emerged in a motorcade and were escorted into town. Fans lined the route from the Parkway West all the way to the Civic Center. Some couldn't believe the Liverpool Lads were finally here.

On the night of the concert some fans were so excited they broke through a police line set up outside the arena. Once inside the anticipation was building. Fans were first treated to some opening acts which included: Clarence "Frogman" Henry, Jackie DeShannon, the Exciters and the Bill Black Combo. Once the Beatles did appear, pandemonium erupted. The frenzied sold-out crowd of 12,603 yelled and screamed constantly. Reports show that the concert had to be stopped numerous times as the police came on stage and pleaded for some order. After the half hour show, things were not much better. Rumor has it the "Fab Four" had to leave the arena in an ambulance. Were they injured? No, they just needed an inconspicuous escape! By the way, this was the first and only time the Beatles played at the Civic Arena.

Did you know before the Beatles came to town, Pittsburgh Police watched television footage of a Beatles concert in San Francisco? They were specifically looking for techniques on crowd control.

37) December 28

"You Got IT"

On this evening KQV radio station presented their Christmas Shower of Stars. The headliners were smooth singing Roy Orbison, Jackie "Mr. Excitement" Wilson and an all-girl teenage group from New York called The Shangri-Las.

At the time Orbison was a veteran of the music business and had hits like: Running Scared, Dream Baby, Crying, Candy Man, Workin' For the Man, In

Dreams, Blue Bayou, It's Over, and the ever popular Oh, Pretty Woman. Jackie Wilson was no slouch either. He could sing but danced with the best of them- thus the nickname "Mr. Excitement". His popular songs included: My Empty Arms, Doggin' Around, Night, Baby Workout, Alone At Last, To Be Loved, That's Why, I'll Be Satisfied and Lonely Teardrops. The Shangri-Las, named after a restaurant in Queens, New York, had a 'tough –girls' persona. Their smash hit Leader of the Pack exemplified this image. Other offerings in their repertoire were: Simon Says, Wishing Well, Hate to Say I Told You So and favorite Remember (Walking in the Sand)

Did you know the Christmas Shower of Stars show was so popular it broke a Civic Arena attendance record? Around 14,000 people came out during this holiday-time break thus beating the old record by 330.

1965

38) February 5-7

Jobs and leisure under one roof

For three days the Civic Arena opened its doors to the first ever Career Exposition. A couple significant things about this event were: the attendance figures and other events simultaneously taking place. The Exposition, which was mainly a showcase of opportunities for youth and retraining of adults, at- tracted 36,630 people! At the time, this would have equaled about 3 sold-out hockey games. However, while many folks were filing through the many rooms of the "Igloo" thinking of work, others had fun on their minds. On the evening of February 5 the ice surface of the Civic Arena was converted into an indoor auto racing track. Three Quarter (TQ) midgets were the special guests and the 4,500 fans in attendance ate it up. The TQ which are even smaller than the conventional midgets competed in an eight-event program. Drivers raced on a high-banked one-tenth mile oval. Winners received points that went toward the season standings. The final race was special as it featured local drivers. The winner was Norm Benning from Braddock.

On February 6, the Civic Arena had one of its busiest days ever. While the Career Exposition was in full swing, the ice surface saw three activities that day. First it started with some leisure public ice skating from 1:30 to 4:30pm. Then at 8:00pm things got a little more intense. The Pittsburgh Hornets took on the powerful Rochester Americans in AHL action. After battling for over 2 hours, the sting had been taken out of the Hornets and the first place Americans went on to victory. Disappointment filled the air but the night wasn't over yet. At 10:30 pm another ice battle started. This time it featured the Pittsburgh Knights and the New York Flyers from the Mid-Atlantic Hockey League.

Maybe Pittsburgh fans left over from the Hornet game would see a better result this time. Well it didn't take long before pucks were filling the net. Fortunately for the Knights, they were getting the majority of goals. As the night wore on the Flyers faded like an old pair of jeans. When the final buzzer sounded Pittsburgh had crushed New York 21 to 3. The 21 goals by the Knights were a league record along with the 6 unassisted goals by Ron Mason. Why such a lop-sided defeat? It probably had to do with the fact New York arrived in Pittsburgh with only 7 players!

39) March 4

The run is finally over!

In high school basketball action a crowd of 9,620 witnessed the Aliquippa Quips pull off one of the biggest upsets of the year. They defeated the Uniontown Red Raiders 66 to 65 in the semi-finals of the Western Pennsylvania Inter-Athletic League (WPIAL) playoffs. Uniontown had been the1964 AAA Pennsylvania State Champions and were riding a 2-year 52-game winning streak!

The Quips started the game employing a man-to-man defense that stymied the top Raider shooters. In fact, by half-time Aliquippa led by 14 while limiting Uniontown to just 22 points. In the third quarter, while still using a full-court press Uniontown forced Aliquippa to make some bad shots and passes. The Raiders kept chipping away at the ominous lead. By the last quarter they tied the score and then briefly went ahead by a bucket. Aliquippa was now in for a fight and dug in their heels. They responded with some key baskets while Uniontown missed a few. In the dying seconds Aliquippa held on and beat the mighty Raiders by 1 point.

Aliquippa's starting five played the whole game and each reached double digits. They were led by Chad Calabria with 18 then Gary Davies 15, Bob Chenet 12, Chris Peacock 11 and Joe Lecee with 10. Despite their Herculian efforts this day, the Quips were not able to duplicate their success. They lost the WPIAL Finals to Midland 62 to 41. Midland's Simmie Hill scored an amazing 38 points-a record at the time.

Did you know the longest winning streak was 54 games held by the Darby-Colwyn Rams of Delaware County in the south east region of Pennsylvania?

40) March 25

The beginning of a hoops tradition

Were you there for the first ever Dapper Dan Roundball Classic? This annual high school All-Star basketball game pitted the best players from Pennsylvania against the U.S. All-Stars. Its originator, John Paul "Sonny" Vaccaro from the Pittsburgh area was himself a high school basketball coach. At the time Vaccaro saw Western Pennsylvania as a hotbed for football but wanted a showcase for basketball stars. Thus the Roundball Classic was conceived and for the next 27 years the Pittsburgh Civic Arena saw some of the best players ever to play the game. In fact many of them went on to brilliant NBA careers (i.e. Kobe Bryant, Moses Malone, Shaquille O'Neal etc.).

On the night of the first Classic, the city of Pittsburgh pulled out all the stops. First, the anticipation of the game alone led to a sold-out crowd of 10,334. Second, Mayor Joseph M. Barr was an invited guest and threw out the first ball. Third, at half-time, the Miss Roundball Classic was crowned. Andrea Krol, an Ambridge High Senior was the winner. Fourth, throughout the game, music was provided by the Mt. Lebanon High band. Lastly, cheerleading came from Robert Morris Junior College in the form of the Steelerettes. Yes, the Steelerettes were indeed the Pittsburgh Steelers cheerleaders. They formed in the early 1960's and were part of the team for almost a decade. During their off time, the Steelerettes cheered at various basketball games and made public appearances.

Meanwhile back to the game itself. In the first half both teams battled hard as baskets were evenly exchanged. However, in the third period the Pennsylvania All-Stars blew the game open when they went on a 12-point run. In the end this proved to be the difference as they beat the U.S. All-Stars 89-76. Sam Hill, Midland's All-State, All-America was the top scorer with 28 points and was named Pennsylvania's M.V.P. His Midland teammates, Brown and Vanlier pitched in 11 and 10 points respectively. Other sharpshooters for the hometown Pennsylvania team were Pat Yates (Uniontown star) with18 and Dick Braucher (Kutztown) with15.

Did you know before the Roundball Classic was played a preliminary one was contested? In that game the City-Catholic All-Stars defeated the West Penn. All-Stars 70-69 when Schenley's Archie McGill scored on a last second jump shot.

41) May 31

Gentlemen start your engines.

On this day race car fans came out to the Civic Arena to see a closed -circuit telecast of the famous Indy 500. The field of 33 racers included: 31 Americans, 1 Canadian and 1 Scottish driver. Big names like Al and Bobby Unser, A.J. Foyt and Pennsylvania's favorite son Mario Andretti were all vying for the win. As the race started, cars jockeyed for position. Soon a leader would emerge. That would be Jim Clarke (the lone Scotsman) and he was gaining time as the 200-lap race developed. No one else gained momentum. As the pressure mounted some cars started bowing out. When the final flag was waved Clarke in his 4.2 liter Ford engined Lotus 38 cruised to victory. Not only had he won the "brickyard" classic but for the first time in Indy history he had averaged a speed of 150 mph. Parnelli Jones finished second while Andretti in his Brawner Hawk finished third. For Andretti he would go on to win the Rookie of the Year Award.

Did you know Jim Clarke captured the 1963 and 1965 Formula One World Championships? Did you also know he was leading the 1964 Indy 500 but bowed out because of suspension problems?

42) June 2 and June 5

The Pink Panther comes to the Igloo

On these two nights Pittsburgh music fans got a real treat. Starting June 2 the Pittsburgh Symphony made local history by performing its first ever Promenade Concert at the Civic Arena. As an added bonus the conductor that night was world renowned local boy Henry Mancini. Mancini who was raised in the steel town of West Aliquippa, Pennsylvania led the Symphony in such hits as: Days of Wine and Roses, The Baby Elephant Walk, Moon River and of course Pink Panther. A few days later Pittsburgh was privileged again to see the Symphony at the Igloo. This time it was led by another famous conductor in the name of New Yorker Morton Gould.

Did you know part of the set up for these concerts consisted of two hundred tables (each seating four persons) placed on the Civic Arena floor?

43) June 18-20

The best ever assembled?

For Pittsburgh Jazz fans this might have been the closest to heaven on earth. This tree-day Jazz Festival had some of the finest players ever assembled. The line-up included: the Walt Harper Quintet, The Earl Hines Trio, Carmen McRae and her Trio, The Stan Getz Quartet with Gary Burton, The John Coltrane Quartet (with McCoy Tyner, Jimmy Garrison and Elvin Jones) the Duke Ellington Orchestra, Count Bassie, Miles Davies, Dizzy Gillespie, Woody Herman and Muddy Waters. For some young fans in attendance, these outstanding performances were the spark which led them into jazz careers.

Did you know Bill Kirchner who is a present day saxophonist, composer, arranger, bandleader, record and radio producer, jazz historian and educator was in attendance as a young boy on June 19th?

44) November 10

A champion boxer is finished

In somewhat of a sad night at the Civic Arena, 27 year-old boxer Joey Archer beat the sweetness out of "Sugar" Ray Robinson (44) in a lop-sided 10th round decision. Robinson, though tough, was on the defense most of the night. He even received a standing nine-count in the fourth round when Archer knocked him to the canvas. For the 9,023 in attendance, they would witness something historical. This would turn out to be Robinson's 200th fight and final one as a professional. After the bout while in the dressing room, Miles Davis, the musician, told Robinson "Sugar, its time man." The next day Robinson announced his retirement and was quoted as saying "I hate to go too long campaigning for another chance."

Did you know "Sugar "Ray Robinson won 173 of his 200 career fights? In many circles he has been cited as the greatest boxer of all time.

45) November 24

The Stones do it right this time

KQV Thanksgiving Shower of Stars presented the Rolling Stones (I Can't Get No Satisfaction), The Byrds (Mr. Tambourine Man), We Five (You Were On My Mind), Bo Diddley (You Can't Judge a Book By the Cover), The Vibrations (My Girl Sloopy), Paul Revere and the Raiders (Steppin' Out and

Just Like Me) and Simon and Garfunkel (The Sound of Silence). Quite a lineup for one evening!

For the Stones, this was their second go-around to the Steel City. Unfortunately, in their first gig at the West View Park Danceland on June 17, 1964 they drew a scantily 250 people. This night was a whole different story as the Civic Arena was packed (9,131) to the rafters. Fans coming out to this multi-billed show certainly got a taste of different music genres.

Did you know tickets for the Thanksgiving Shower of Stars ranged from $3.00 to $5.00?

1961

1. Mary Brignano, *Pittsburgh Civic Light Opera: How the Dreams Came True*. Sewickley, PA: White Oak Publishing, 1996

1. Pittsburgh Post-Gazette, September 18, 1961

2. http://www.pittsburghhockey.net/Common/CivicArena/CivicArena.html

2. Pittsburgh Post-Gazette, September 17&19, 1961

3. Pittsburgh Post-Gazette, September 24 and November 21, 1961

4. http://www.pittsburghhockey.net/HornetsPages/HornetsTIME1.html

4. http://en.wikipedia/BuffaloBisons_(AHL)

5. http://www.steelbeltwrestling.com/index.php?option=com_content&task=view&id=108&Itemid=44

6. http://www.post-gazette.com/pg/04298/401075-158.stm

6. http://hipbopper.peopleaggregator.net/showcontent.php?tag_id=5182

7. www.geocities.com/Heartland/6046/larells.html

7. oldmonmusic.blogspot.com/2008/07/la-rells.html

8. http://www.nba.com/history/this_date_november

8. Pittsburgh Post-Gazette, November 8, 1961

9. Indiana Evening Gazette, November 24, 1961

9. Pittsburgh Post-Gazette, November, 1961

10. Sam Sciullo, Jr., Sam Sciullo. *Pitt: 100 years of Pitt Basketball*. Sports Publishing LLC, 2005

11. http://www.boxrec.com/list_bouts.php?human_id=009625&cat=boxer

11. Indiana Evening Gazette, November 24, 1961

11. http://www.cmgworldwide.com/sports/robinson/biography.html

12. Pittsburgh Post-Gazette, December 17, 1961

1962

13. Pittsburgh Post-Gazette, January 8, 1962 page 23

14. Pittsburgh Post-Gazette, January 16, 1962

15. Pittsburgh Post-Gazette, February 22, 1962, page 26

16. www.apbr.org/ablhist.html

16. http://members.aol.com/bradleyrd/ablhist.html

16. Pittsburgh Post-Gazette March 30, 1962 page 17&20

17. Pittsburgh Post-Gazette, April 23, 1962 page 1&12

18. Pittsburgh Post-Gazette, May 3, 1962 page 25

19. http://www.440.com/_pchedw.html

19. http://wwwpbrtv.com/porky.html

20. Pittsburgh Post-Gazette May 11& June 1, 1962

21. www.post-gazette.com/localnews/20020513arena0513p2.asp

21. Mary Brignano. *Pittsburgh Civic Light Opera: How the Dreams Came True*. Op. cit.

22. Pittsburgh Post-Gazette, July 9, 1962 page 4

23. Mary Brignano, *Pittsburgh Civic Light Opera: How the Dreams Came True*. Op. cit.

24. Mary Brignano, *Pittsburgh Civic Light Opera: How the Dreams Came True*. Op. cit.

25. Mary Brignano, *Pittsburgh Civic Light Opera: How the Dreams Came True*. Op. cit.

1963

26. http://www.pittsburghhockey.net/HornetsPages/HornetsVersus.html

26. http://enwikipedia.org/wiki/1962-63_NHL_season

27. Pittsburgh Post-Gazette, January 21, 1963, page 22

28. http://www.boxing-memorabilia.com/biopowell.htm

28. Pittsburgh Post-Gazette, January 25, 1963 page 18&19

29. Pittsburgh Post Gazette, March 13, 1963

30. www.com/the-perry-como-show/show/...summary.html

30. www.ataudio.com/ata_search_as.php?QS...perry%20como

31. http://espn.go.com/classic/s/000731hurricaneadd.html

31. Pittsburgh Post-Gazette, December 21, 1963

1964

32. http://www.pittsburghhockey.net/HornetsPages/HornetsSeasons/63-64CAP.html

33. Deanna R. Adams. *Rock 'N' Roll and the Cleveland Connection*. Kent State University Press, 2002

33. Pittsburgh Post Gazette, June 6, 1964

34. Pittsburgh Post-Gazette, June 22, 1964 page 1

35. http://craftonreunion.org/home/id77.html

35. Pittsburgh Post Gazette, August 13, 1964

36. http://www.geocities.com/~Beatleboy1/db1964.0914.beatles.html

36. http://www.post-gazette.com/magazine/20001208BeatleSide5.asp

36. Lynn Cowden-one of the fans at the concert (personal interview)

37. http://user.pa.net/~ejjeff/timeline.html

1965

38. http://user.pa.net/~ejjeff/timeline.html

39. Pittsburgh Post-Gazette, March 5, 1965

40. Pittsburgh Post-Gazette, March 26, 1965.

41. http://www.1-18scalecars.com/OLotus_38_1965_Indy_500_winner.htm

41. http://www.jeromegoolsby.net/racing.html

41. http://www.themotorsportgallery.co.uk/mg-ford-tribute.htm

41. http://www.post-gazette.com/pg07021/755217-85stm

42. Pittsburgh Post-Gazette, June 3&6, 1965

43. http://www.depanorama.net/1960s2htm

43. htttp://www.jerryjazzmusician.com/main HTML.cfm?page=tempo-7.html

44. http://www.hotboxingnews.com/mccoy050703.htm

44. http://www.gov-certificates.co.uk/birth/certificate/Sugar_Ray_Robinson

45. http://user.pa.net/`ejjeff/kqvconcerts.html

Chapter 2, 1966-1970

1966

<u>46) March 25&26</u>

The best hardwood players in the state converge at the Igloo

This was the first time the Pennsylvania Inter-scholastic Athletic Association (PIAA) Basketball Championships were held at the Civic Arena since its inception in 1920.

In the first game held March 25th, the Mercer Mustangs took on the Darby-Colwyn Rams in the AA final. From the opening tip-off both teams battled hard. The action was fast and furious and the lead kept going back and forth. By the start of the fourth quarter neither team distinguished themselves as the dog fight continued. Talk about an even match, when the final buzzer sounded the score was tied. As overtime started the Mustang record of 27 and 0 was on the line. In the extra frame no one gave an inch either. However, pumped up by the mostly pro-Mercer fans, the Mustangs found another gear. They drained some critical baskets and hung on to win. The final score was 55 to 52. The Civic Arena crowd had just witnessed one of the closest PIAA games in history.

The next day 10,541 hoops fans came to see the Schenley Spartans (Pittsburgh) take on the Chester Clippers (Philadelphia) in the elite AAA final. The pro-Schenley crowd cheered on their boys all the way. Again it was a heated game with players taking a lot of punishment under the basket. Spartan star Ken Durett had a decent first half scoring 16 points. However, mid-way through the third quarter his luck ran out. Taking his 4th personal foul, the coach benched him. The rest of the boys, shaken, responded with fire. Montel Brundage led Schenley and scored a team-high 22 points. Meanwhile teammate Marvin Snowden picked up his game and finished the night with 16 points and a game-high 14 rebounds. By the time the final horn sounded, Schenley had won comfortably 74 to 64.

Did you know the Spartans' victory was their first state title in school history?

47) December 10

The city starts a new tournament tradition

Were you there when the Civic Arena hosted its first ever Steel Bowl basketball tournament? The tournament which started in the early 1950's, pitted the city teams Duquesne Dukes and Pittsburgh Panthers against two outside teams. Winners would play in the final while losers played a consolation game.

On this day Duquesne would claim city superiority by beating the Panthers 72 to 65. However, the Dukes couldn't brag too much because it was only the consolation final! The tournament final saw Ivy League boys Columbia (N.Y.) Edge Indiana State 63 to 59.

Did you know in the 9 years the Steel Bowl was played at the Civic Arena, Duquesne beat Pittsburgh 7 times?

48) December 30

Is this some kind of "Monkey" business?

On this second last day of 1966, the KQV Christmas Shower of Stars presented The Monkees. If you were at this concert early, you may have recalled what radio announcer Hal Murray was wearing when he introduced the band. He was decked out in his Emperor's Cape while holding a scepter.

As for The Monkees, they were formed in 1965 strictly as a made for television band. This, to a large part, was a response to the Beatles' release of the film "Hard Day's Night" in 1964. Though the Monkees boasted some great individual musicians it was their television show that rocketed the group to a whole new level. Aired from September 12, 1966 to March 25, 1968 it made Davy and the boys household names to millions of people. In the show, the lads were always up to some crazy antics and in the process made them more endearing to us.

At the Civic Arena show, Mickey Dolenz, Peter Tork, Davy Jones and Michael Nesmith interspersed their signature style humor throughout the show. Most fans new the words to every song including: I'm a Believer, Last Train to Clarksville, Daydream Believer, and (I'm Not Your) Stepping Stone etc. and sang along with the band.

Did you know one of the Monkees hits "I'm a Believer" was written by Neil Diamond? Did you also know that the mother of band member Michael Nesmith invented the office product Liquid Paper? She later sold her company to Gillette in 1979 for 47 million dollars.

1967

49) February 17

Roller Derby kings and queens

On this night Pittsburgh got a taste of a different sport. Were you there to see live roller derby with all its bumping and bashing? A curious sellout crowd of 10,676 gathered at the Civic Arena. Others arriving too late were turned away at the door. Nonetheless, the two teams who had met in the final of the Roller Derby League the year before readied for action. They were the New York Chiefs and the San Francisco Bombers (defending champions).

When the whistle blew the game started fast and furious. Bodies were flying all over the place and the audience lapped it up. The hard hitting match saw the lead change several times. As the game winded down the Bombers dug a little deeper as they kept up the pressure. It certainly paid off as they eked out a 35 to 31 win.

Did you know the New York Chiefs boasted three unusual players? The first was Ronnie Robinson the son of former world boxing champion Sugar Ray Robinson. The second and third were Mike Gammon and Judy McGuire the only man and wife combination in the league.

50) February 24

The Big Dipper breaks another record

Were you there when the Philadelphia 76'ers destroyed the Baltimore Bullets 149-118 in NBA action? Playing for the winning team, Wilt "The Stilt" chamberlain pumped in 42 points. Though pretty impressive, it was how the big man scored that got him some notoriety. He broke a league record by shooting

18 consecutive field goals. "The Stilt" was so hot; he didn't miss a basket all night! Later, in a following game, Chamberlain would extend his streak to 35.

Though the Baltimore Bullets lost this night, one of their players received special recognition. At half-time, Jack Marin, a former Farrell high school star and All American at Duke University received a plaque from the mayor of Farrell. The appreciative crowd of 8,642 gave their home town boy a warm applause. Marin, who was a NBA rookie, would go on to score 17 points in the game.

In a preliminary game that night Point Park College beat the Westminster Jayvees in a squeaker 67-65.

Did you know in the 1967 NBA Finals the Philadelphia 76ers defeated the San Francisco Warriors 4 games to 2? Did you also know Wilt Chamberlain once scored 100 points in one night? It occurred on March 2, 1962 when his Philadelphia Warriors beat the New York Knicks 169 to 147. The game was played in Hershey, Pennsylvania.

51) February 26

Can you smell the rubber?

Racing fans gathered at the Igloo to see the Ninth Annual Daytona 500 on Closed Circuit television. This was special as individuals, who would normally watch the event on private televisions, experienced a crowd atmosphere. Furthermore, this would be a historical night being that it was the first ever closed circuit telecast of the famed race. In all, a half a million people around the world saw the race including 100,000 live at the Daytona race track. The winner was Mario Andretti driving a Ford 67. He collected $43,000 for his efforts.

Did you know Mario Andretti was born in Italy but was raised in Nazareth, Pennsylvania and still lives there today?

52) March 30

Is this the short and sweet science?

On this night 32 year-old Floyd Patterson (45-5), a former two-time heavyweight champion of the world took on Bill McMurray. Patterson was anxious to get another title shot though some critics said he was too old. It didn't take him very long to silence the naysayers when he knocked out the two-hundred and nine pound McMurray at 2:37 of the first round. Just 2 seconds before this, McMurray was leveled to the canvas and barely survived a standing 8-count. Patterson sensing victory went in for the kill.

Did you know Floyd Patterson lost his last pro fight to Ali on September 20, 1972?

53) April 8

Moonlighting cheerleaders get a bonus

Henry Mancini and Andy Williams teamed up for a performance with the Pittsburgh Symphony. Fans of the leading conductor (Mancini) and the ever popular singer (Williams) were delighted that they got two for the price of one. The dynamic combination hit a high note when Williams sang Mancini's famed Days of Wine and Roses. As an added bonus fans got to see special guests the Steelerettes. Yes these were the Pittsburgh Steelers cheerleaders and some were invited to perform. They actually provided the stage backdrop for "Watching All The Girls Go By" sung by Mr. Williams. After the show, the cheerleaders got a thrill of a lifetime when they met Mancini and Williams and received autographed albums from them.

Did you know Henry Mancini grew up in the Pittsburgh area? His real name was Enrico Nicola Mancini?

54) April 30

It was the icing on the cake!

On this spring night, the Pittsburgh Hornets defeated the Rochester Americans 4-3 in American Hockey League playoff action. The winning goal scored by Billy Harris just 26 seconds into over-time gave the Hornets a four game sweep of the Final Series and their third Calder Cup Championship. Ironically, the winning goal would also be the last one scored in Pittsburgh Hornet history. The Hornets folded after the season just as the city of Pittsburgh was awarded an NHL franchise.

Did you know the losing Rochester Americans boasted 2 defensemen who would later become successful NHL coaches? Their names were Al Arbour and Don Cherry.

55) June 9-11

The Civic Arena opens its doors to the world

Were you there when the International Pittsburgh Folk Festival came to the Civic Arena for the first time since its inception in 1956? On these 3 days, twenty-three countries showed off their displays and costumes. In addition there was music and dancing demonstrations as well as food from the four corners of the world. Over 30,000 customers attended the 3-day festival.

The first dance performance of the festival was provided by the Batya Fisher folk festival troupe. The accompanying songs, originating from Israeli included: "Bat Szurim" a sweetheart dance, "Shir Ha-Botzrim" a rejoicing dance representing vintners after a good grape crop and "Sherele" a fun dance meaning scissors.

Did you know the International Pittsburgh Folk Festival still takes place presently? Its' new home is the David Lawrence Convention Center.

56) June 25

Who's your mama?

The KQV Super Summer Spectacular presented The Mama's and the Papa's with guest stars The Buckinghams and The Moby Grape. As one of the hottest groups of their time, The Mama's and the Papa's was the quintessential 1960's hippie band. Their songs included California Dreamin and Monday, Monday. Speaking about Monday, Monday you may recall the surprised shock on Mama Cass Elliot's face as she started to sing this song the night of this concert. Why? The roof of the Civic Arena was opening up.

Did you know a week before their visit to Pittsburgh, The Mama's and the Papa's performed at the famed Monterey International Pop Festival in California? Other artists at the gathering included the likes of Jefferson Airplane, The Who, The Jimi Hendrix Experience and Big Brother &The Holding Company featuring Janis Joplin-not bad company if you ask me!

57) July 10-15

Jacks are wild!

On these warm summer nights the Pittsburgh Civic Light Opera (CLO) presented The Jack Benny Revue. This was the CLO's first set of shows in its

6th season at the Civic Arena. As a veteran comedian in television and radio, Benny kept his audiences in stitches with his signature delayed-style jokes and stories. At one point he even took out his beloved violin to play a couple tunes. Though not very proficient, he used the instrument more to get timely laughs.

Special guest to the performances was co-star/singer Jack Jones. Jones delighted the audience with a mix of tunes. Fan favorites included: Sound of Music medley hits, Wives and Lovers, Lollipops and Roses, The Race is On, The Impossible Dream (The Quest) and Donkey Serenade-a hit song for his father, Allan Jones. Much later in his career (1980), Jack would sing "The Love Boat Theme."

Did you know while in Pittsburgh Jack Benny played in the Fifth Annual Ham-Am golf tournament at Churchill Valley Country Club? At one point during the tourney Jack lay on his back and placed a tee in his mouth. Then Arnold Palmer placed a ball on it and took a whack! Needless to say the anxious gallery got a chuckle.

58) August 28-September 2

A superstar is even impressed!

For six evenings in a row the Civic Arena was filled with music from one of the flashiest entertainers of his era. Audiences got to hear and see Mr. "Showmanship" himself-Liberace. On opening night the flamboyant performer had the crowd hooked from the beginning wearing a pink sequined suit. Later he changed into a white one then a black one that he claimed cost $10,000 because of the studded diamonds. Beyond the extravagant costumes Liberace kept spectators eyes glued to him with his music and self-deprecating jokes. His repertoire of hits included: Born Free, Strangers in the Night, Alley Cat, How Insensitive, Mack the Knife, Got Rhythm and Fascination Rhythm. He even spoke the lyrics for The Impossible Dream. Not being shy about his success Liberace often bragged about it in a humorous way. At one point he quipped, "Remember the bank I used to cry all the way to?" "I own it now."

In one of his performances the Civic Arena roof opened up to the delight of the audience. Impressed also by the sight, Liberace stopped playing the piano briefly and said, "I've never seen a more beautiful sight in my life."

Did you know on November 22, 1963 Liberace collapsed after a show at the Holiday House in Pittsburgh? He was brought to St. Francis Hospital and diagnosed with uremic poisoning. The condition, which shut his kidneys down for 14 days, was caused by inhaling carbon tetrachloride fumes used in dry cleaning his costumes. Liberace spent 20 days in the hospital for treatment and recovery.

59) October 11

The beginning of a new hockey era

Were you there to see the Montreal Canadiens defeat the Pittsburgh Penguins 2-1? If so, you were among the 9,307 fans that saw the Penguin's first ever regular season game at the Civic Arena. Also this was the first NHL game played in the city of Pittsburgh since 1930.

Back in the mid-1920's Pittsburgh had an NHL team called the Pirates. They played 5 years in the city before moving to Philadelphia to become the Quakers.

On this opening night in 1967, Andy Bathgate's (former N.Y. Ranger star) goal in the third period would become the first in Penguin franchise history. On the Canadiens side, legendary forward Jean Beliveau made a little history himself when he scored his 400th career goal on Hank Bassen. To date he would become only the third player in the NHL to have reached this milestone. The first two were Maurice Richard and Gordie Howe.

Did you know 4 players on the Penguin team had played for the Pittsburgh Hornets when they won the Calder Cup in the spring of 1967? They were: Val Fonteyne, Ab McDonald, Andy Bathgate and goalie Hank Bassen.

60) October 21

A nice ice breaker

Ten days after their inaugural home opener, the Pittsburgh Penguins doubled up the Chicago Black Hawks 4-2. The victory was the first home win for the Pens in franchise history. Secondly, and just as important, Pittsburgh would also be the first expansion team to beat one of the original six teams.

Before the game Penguins coach Red Sullivan told his player Ken Schinkel to shadow Blackhawk superstar Bobby Hull. It worked out well for Pittsburgh as Hull didn't score once and Schinkel ended up with 3! Chicago, led also by co-star Stan Mikita, started the 1967-68 season with 7 straight losses including this one.

Did you know the 6 new NHL expansion teams were: Philadelphia, Pittsburgh, Los Angeles, California, St. Louis, and Minnesota? The original six NHL teams were: Boston, New York, Toronto, Montreal, Chicago and Detroit.

61) October 24

Basketball returns with a familiar face

In 1967, as hockey started a new era in the Steel City so did basketball. On this night the new Pittsburgh Pipers played their first ever American Basketball Association (ABA) regular season game at the Civic Arena. Their opponents from the North Star state, the Minnesota Muskies, boasted stars like: Mel Daniels, Donnie Freeman and Les Hunter. The Pipers on the other hand, were led by none other than Connie Hawkins. Hawkins would make his second debut with a Pittsburgh basketball team. His first go round came with the Pittsburgh Renaissances (Rens) of the ABL where he captured MVP awards in 1961-62 as a 19 year-old. Other stars on the Pipers were Charlie Williams and Chico Vaughn.

In this game Hawkins led Pittsburgh with 19 points. Unfortunately it wasn't enough as the Muskies scored 34 points in the third period and went on to silence the crowd of 5,719 and Pittsburgh 104-86.

Did you know after playing for the Pittsburgh Rens Connie Hawkins joined the Harlem Globetrotters?

62) December 9

Duquesne hits century mark against city rivals

On this day the Duquesne Dukes men's basketball team could do no wrong. They beat their arch-rivals the Pittsburgh Panthers by a whopping score of 100-66 in the Steel Bowl final game. Led by sophomore Bill Zopf, the Dukes scored 60 points in the second half alone. Zopf would finish the game with 23 points and be named the tournaments' MVP.

Duquesne had reached the finals by defeating Air Force 64-52 while Pittsburgh squeaked by Massachusetts 73-71.

Did you know to date, the Dukes victory in the Steel Bowl finals (100-66) remains the biggest point spread (34) in the history of the Pittsburgh-Duquesne rivalry?

1968

63) February 3

The best come to town

Were you there when the defending Stanley Cup Champions Toronto Maple Leafs paid a visit to the Igloo? Fans were curious to see how their Pittsburgh Penguins would stack up against the best in the league. In fact so many people turned up that it became the first home sold-out game in Penguin franchise history. The official attendance was 12,563. By the way Pittsburgh put on a good show and battled Toronto to a 3-3 draw. Penguin scorers that night were Ab McDonald with 2 and Gene Ubriaco with 1.

Did you know the Pittsburgh Hornets (AHL) who played six years at the Civic Arena never had a sell-out? Did you also know the Toronto Maple Leafs have never won the Stanley Cup since 1967?

64) February 17

Spread the wealth around!

On this night, in front of a sparse crowd of 4,981, the Eastern division leaders Pittsburgh Pipers met the Western division leaders the New Orleans Buccaneers. The two offensive-minded basketball teams combined to score 250 points! Luckily for the home crowd the Pipers won the game 129-121. In a rare feat of consistency, 5 Piper players scored 20 (+) plus points.

Did you know after this season, the Pittsburgh Pipers moved to Minnesota? They became the Minnesota Pipers and played there one year. The following year they returned to Pittsburgh and played 3 more years-the last two of which they were called the Condors.

65) February 21

For Pete's sake!

In NHL action the Pittsburgh Penguins tied the Philadelphia Flyers 1-1. For the first time in their inaugural season, 9,198 Penguin fans got to see the teams' new mascot. His name was "Penguin Pete" and he was a real Ecuadorian-born penguin that lived at the Pittsburgh Aquazoo.

Did you know Penguin President Jack McGregor gave "Penguin Pete" as a present to his son Doug for his ninth birthday?

66) February 26

Some mighty Oaks fall!

In front of a measly crowd of 1,163 the Pittsburgh Pipers defeated the Oakland Oaks 150-126 and in the process make a little team history. First, the 150 points for the Pipers would break their record for most points in a game. Second, the 84 points scored in the second half would beat another record. Third, their 51 points in the 4th quarter was the most ever. Star player Connie Hawkins would once again lead the way with 36 points.

Unfortunately for the Pipers this evening also had some tragedy. Towards the end of the game Jim Hadnot of the Oaks viciously elbowed Piper sub Graig Dill-in the temple. Dill was knocked out and hit the floor in a heap. Once he was attended to, the ambulance quickly whisked him to Mercy Hospital. After some observations and a short stay there, the Piper player recovered and was eventually released.

Did you know three weeks after this game (on March 18, 1968) the Pipers would match their record high points when they demolished the Anaheim Amigos 150 to 122?

67) March 22&23

The Igloo hosts the state championships again

In only the second time in its history the PIAA Basketball Championships were held at the Civic Arena. On the first day 7,313 fans saw 2 games. In the first one, Mount Penn took on Williamsburg in the boys A final. Both teams battled hard throughout the game. As the clock ticked away overtime was looming. Just as the buzzer was ready to sound Bob Romanski of Mount Penn was fouled. At the free throw line he drained both baskets as his team won in a thriller 62 to 61. Romanski was the hero and also led all scorers that day with 24.

On the same day the Middletown Blue Raiders faced East Brady in the boys AA final. This one was no contest as the Blue Raiders led by Dave Twardzik smashed East Brady 78 to 48. Middletown would finish the season with an impressive 28 and 1 record.

On the next day more than 9,500 fans came to see the boys AAA final between the Laurel Highland Mustangs and the Cheltenham Panthers. Like the A final this was a tight game. Both teams didn't give an inch. In the dying seconds Wilbert Robinson of the Mustangs stuffed a shot by Panthers big man Graig Littlepage to preserve a tie. The game would head to overtime. Building on their defensive play Laurel Highlands would go on to win 63 to 56. Wilbert Robinson had 31 points for the winners but his blocked shot at the end of the game was the difference.

Did you know Wilbert Robinson went on to be a star at West Virginia University?

68) May 4

The pinnacle is reached!

Fans gather at the Civic Arena for game 7 of the Finals. Could this be the Pittsburgh Penguins trying to make history in their rookie season? No, this was the Pittsburgh Pipers looking to become the first league champs of the American Basketball Association. In earlier play-off rounds the Pipers disposed of both the Indiana Pacers and the Minnesota Muskies. This time they faced the best team in the West in the New Orleans Buccaneers. The series was tied 3 to 3 so this one was for all the marbles. The game finally started and to the delight of the 11,457 fans, the Pipers took the early lead. They kept pressing and by half-time went to the dressing room ahead 67 to 55. In the third quarter the Pipers stretched their lead to 20 points thanks in large part to the efforts of Charlie Williams. He would have the hot hand and finish the night with 35 points. However, in the fourth quarter the Bucs made their move. Led by Doug Moe, he would bring his team within 5 points not once but 3 times. The Pipers responded and drained a few more baskets. As time ticked away Pittsburgh kept their cool. Finally the buzzer rang and the fans madly celebrated. The Pipers won 122 to 113!

In addition to winning the ABA championships this year, the Pipers also received some individual awards. Connie Hawkins was named the MVP for both the season and the Finals while Vince Cazzetta was named Coach of the Year.

Did you know the New Orleans Buccaneers basketball team was owned by the father of Harry Connick Jr.?

69) October 19

"Penguin Pete" performs for the people

Were you there when the "Big Bad" Boston Bruins humbled the Pittsburgh Penguins 5-1? Before the start of the third period the Pittsburgh mascot, who was a real penguin, led the home team onto the ice. Fans got a good laugh as "Penguin Pete" was actually wearing a pair of skates! The skates were specially made for him by CCM in Canada. "Penguin Pete" had learned to skate from someone at the University of Pittsburgh. After many lessons he made his skating debut.

Unfortunately, about a month after this appearance "Penguin Pete" met an untimely death. On November 23, 1968 he died of all things-pneumonia! Apparently the ice crew at the Civic Arena had kept his nesting area too warm and this proved disastrous for him.

Did you know this was the first Penguin game to be broadcasted on local television (WTAE)?

1969

70) March 28

Defense rules!

Were you there when the Pennsylvania All-Stars defeated the U.S. All-Stars 74-67 in the fifth annual Dapper Dan Roundball Classic (DDRC)? The sold-out crowd (13,380), a Pennsylvania record at the time, witnessed the lowest score ever (both teams) in the history of the game. The win was the first for the Pennsylvania All-Stars since winning the inaugural Dapper Dan Roundball Classic 89-76 in 1965.

Wilkinsburg's 6' 1" Mark "Gino" Gianfrancesco led the Pennsylvanian team with 18 points and was named the team's MVP. The U.S. All-Stars, with their height advantage, were favored to win but couldn't contain the Pennsylvania outside sharp shooters. Nick Weatherspoon from nearby Ohio (Canton McKinley High) did have a good game with 14 points and 17 rebounds and was awarded the MVP for the losing U.S. team.

If you were at the game this evening you might remember how things got under way. Center High's 100-piece band got the crowd riled up as players from a preliminary contest were introduced. In this game the City-Catholic All-Stars took on the West Penn. All-Stars. In one of the best come-from-behind victories of the DDRC, City –Catholic eked out a 93-89 overtime victory. This was the first ever Roundball Classic game, albeit a preliminary one, decided in overtime.

Did you know the Dapper Dan Roundball Classic which started in 1965 was played for 28 consecutive years at the Pittsburgh Civic Arena?

71) July 21-26

The final curtain call for the CLO

On these six evenings, the Pittsburgh Civic Light Opera presented the production of How Now, Dow Jones. The star of this show, Tony Randall, would later become famous on television with the "Odd Couple".

In a scary moment during the July 22 performance, Randall actually injured himself. It occurred as he was running off stage. Apparently he hit his foot on one of the wagons which carried the sets for How Now, Dow Jones. Luckily he was not severely hurt and was able to finish the rest of the shows.

One of the highlights of this production was the number "Step to the Rear" provided by five ladies over the age of 40. They were all members of the Central Park West Canasta and Stock Society.

As Tony Randall's leading lady in these musical shows, Marilyne Mason had a Pittsburgh connection. Her parents were from Greentree and her sister lived in Mt. Lebanon. Arlene Fontana also starred in the show.

Unfortunately for the Civic Light Opera this was their last production at the Civic Arena. Because of poor acoustics (especially when the roof was open) the Civic Light Opera moved to their new home at Heinz Hall.

Did you know Jack Klugman who was the other half of the Odd Couple was at one time a drama student at Carnegie Tech?

72) November 28

You tell them Janis!

On this night Janis Joplin performed a concert with her Kozmic Blues band. At one moment during the show fans started to rush the stage. Civic Arena officials, sensing danger, quickly flicked on the house lights and warned people to be seated or the concert would not continue. Joplin, who was upset about the decision, yelled into microphone "Turn those f*****g lights off." Instantly the place went dark again.

Did you know Janis Joplin died (October 4, 1970) of a drug overdose less than year after this concert? She was 27 years old.

73) December 1

A record comes on the hard court.

Were you there when the Duquesne Dukes men's basketball team broke a school scoring record? With a home crowd of 5, 087 cheering on, they whipped the St.Vincent Bearcats in a romp. The final score was 123-55.

With the fourth quarter winding down, word on the Dukes bench started to spread regarding the previous record. Players wanting to make a little history responded with a flurry of points. In fact in the last 1:50 seconds Duquesne went on a 14 to 2 run. They shattered their previous high of 109 by 14 points. In total 13 Duquesne players scored at least one basket.

Did you know Duquesne's previous high mark of 109 points was accomplished twice? The first was on February 18, 1953 against Geneva and the second was on March 6, 1968 against St. Francis of Loreto.

74) December 20

Was that a great game "Orr" not?

Hockey fans got a taste of greatness when the Boston Bruins disposed of the Pittsburgh Penguins 6-4. Number 4 Bobby Orr of the Big Bad Bruins put on an offensive display as he collected 5 assists in the game.

In the 1969-70 season Orr would become the first defenseman in NHL history to win the scoring race. He scored 33 goals and added 87 assists (NHL record at the time) for 120 points. Furthermore he capped off the year in dramatic fashion by scoring the winning overtime goal in Game 4 of the Stanley Cup Finals. "The Goal" as most hockey fans called it, shows Orr flying through the air after being tripped by St.Louis defenseman Noel Picard. Upon crashing to the ice, teammates jump on him in celebration of their victory.

Did you know the evening before this game the Penguins conducted a "Score A Goal" competition at the Monroeville Mall Ice Palace? Penguin players such as Jean Pronovost, Michel Briere, Al Smith, Jim Morrison and Bob Woytowich were on hand to play with local fans. Special guest that night was opposition player Mr. Robert Orr.

75) December 30

Double dipping

Fans of basketball got to see something unusual at the Civic Arena. They witnessed 2 American Basketball Association (ABA) games played by 4 teams on the same day. In the first game the Indiana Pacers took care of the Miami Floridians 118-109 while in the second one, the home town Pittsburgh Pipers got by the Carolina Cougars 97-89. This would be the first ABA doubleheader played at the Civic Arena.

Did you know two other ABA doubleheaders would occur at the Civic Arena? They both happened in 1971 when the Pittsburgh team would be called the Condors. The first game occurred on January 19 when the Floridians beat the New York Nets 112-107 and the Condors dumped the Carolina Cougars 136-125. A couple weeks later the Floridians defeated the Carolina Cougars 110-102 while the Condors swept pass the New York Nets 119-111.

1970

76) March 30

Was there a "Whole Lotta Love?"

The hard-rocking British band Led Zeppelin made their Civic Arena debut on this night. From all accounts it was a pretty rough and rowdy affair. At one point spectators were getting wild so Plant and the boys walked off stage. This reduced tensions for awhile but it wasn't enough. Afterwards Civic Arena officials cut the concert short for fear of a riot.

77) April 8

Penguins seal the deal

On this night the Pittsburgh Penguins faced the Oakland Seals. This was a historical contest being the first play-off game in Penguin franchise history. In addition, Pittsburgh Mayor, Peter F. Flaherty declared April 8, 1970 as "Pittsburgh Penguins Day." Finally, in their 3rd NHL season, the Penguins would see post-season action.

The Penguins opened the scoring early this night as Jean Pronovost scored on a power play just 65 seconds into the game. Not to be outdone, the Seals notched the game at 1 when Gary Ehman scored on a power play just 8 minutes later. With neither team scoring in the second period, the final frame would decide the game. With the crowd of 8,051 getting anxious the Pens stormed the opposition net and scored at 12:47. Nick Harbaruk would get credit for the goal but Seal goalie Gary Smith was enraged. He jumped to his skates, threw his stick and gloves to the ice and chased the referee with vengeance. As fellow teammates joined him, they argued the goal was no good because a Penguin player (Glen Sather) was in the crease. After the referees deliberated, they concluded the player was in the crease but he was pushed in. Hence, the goal was legitimate. The Penguins were ahead but the game wasn't over yet. Later, with 55 seconds left in the game, the Seals pulled their goalie for an extra attacker. The action was frantic as fans held their breath. The Seals pressed hard to score but couldn't get the equalizer. Penguins won 2-1 in a thriller.

Pittsburgh would eventually go on to sweep the Seals 4 games to 0. In the next round they would be beaten by the St. Louis Blues 4 games to 2 thus preventing their first appearance in a Stanley Cup Final.

Did you know Yogi Berra and his New York Mets along with some Pittsburgh Pirate players were in the audience this night?

78) May 2

The Civic Arena opens its "Doors"

On this night the Doors pleased their fans with an excellent show. From all accounts the charismatic but controversial Jim Morrison was in fine form. The band also recorded the concert and later used three songs (Back Door Man, Love Hides and Five To One) from this gig to appear on their "Absolutely Live" album which was released in July, 1970. On March 4, 2008 the band released a sixteen song CD called The Doors: Live in Pittsburgh 1970. Now fans can have all the songs from that May concert!

Did you know Jim Morrison was married to Patricia Kennealy on June 24, 1970? Unfortunately, just over a year later (July 3, 1971) Morrison passed away in Paris, France.

79) October 10

We just got buffaloed!

Pittsburgh hockey fans got to see a brand new NHL team this evening. They were the Buffalo Sabres who played their first ever regular season game in franchise history. The Sabres were pretty impressive in their debut and beat the Penguins 2-1. Rookie star and future hall of fame player Gilbert Perreault scored the Sabres winning goal.

Did you know what happened during the first intermission of this game? The Penguins introduced their second team mascot. Their first mascot "Pete", a real penguin, had died of pneumonia. He was replaced by a new penguin called "Re-Pete!"

80) November 12

One Condor was flying high tonight

In basketball action the Indiana Pacers defeated the Pittsburgh Condors 135-132 in front of just 2,884 spectators. In this high scoring game, 6'4" second-year Condor, John Brisker scored an amazing 53 points. He went 20 for 36 including 10 free throws and 3, 3 pointers. Yes, the American Basketball Association (ABA) introduced 3 pointers long before the National Basketball Association (NBA) adopted them. The ABA also played with red, white and blue basketballs.

Did you know John Brisker played 3 years in Pittsburgh and later another 3 for the Seattle Supersonics of the NBA?

81) November 17

It smells like desperation

Were you there when the Floridians defeated the Pittsburgh Condors 122-116? The game itself was fairly normal but what happened prior was interesting. In order to boost sagging attendance, Condors' general manager decided to give away all available tickets to this game-that is 13,000 freebies! Only 8,074 fans showed up. In addition, even 3,000 season ticket-holders didn't make an appearance.

82) November 20

El Condor pasa?

On this evening the Virginia Squires pasted the Pittsburgh Condors 151-113. The 151 Squire points would be the most scored by any Condor opponent while playing at the Civic Arena. This would also be the Condors biggest home loss (by 38 points) in their short history. Rookie Charles Scott led the Squires with 41 points while George Carter and Mike Maloy had 31 and 15 respectively. Condors got 23 points from George Thompson while John Brisker contributed 20.

Did you know 6'7" Mike Maloy (Davidson) had been the Condors first round draft pick the year before? Pittsburgh released him because he was overweight.

83) December 30

It feels like a pack of sardines

On this night the powerful UCLA Bruins defeated the Pittsburgh Panthers 77-64 in the Steel Bowl Championship game. The attendance of 13,535 was the largest to date to watch a basketball game in Pittsburgh. Just the day before, the Panthers surprised Duquesne 70 to 58 to end the Dukes 20-game win streak at the Civic Arena.

Did you know UCLA would win the national championships this year? Led by legendary coach John "Wizard of Westwood" Wooden, the Bruins would go 29-1 and beat Villanova 68-62 in the finals.

1966

46. http://www.piaa.org/championships/archive/default.aspx

46. http://www.pahoops.org/records.html

46. http://eteamz.active.com/chesterclippers/index.cfm?

47. Pittsburgh Post-Gazette, December 11, 1966

48. user.pa.net/~ejjeff/kqvconcerts.html

48. www.t.v.com/monkees/show/show/1678/summary.html

48. http://www.answers.com/topic/the-monkees

1967

49. Pittsburgh Post-Gazette, February 18, 1967 page 14

50. Wayne Lynch, *Season of the 76 Ers: The Story of Wilt Chamberlain and the 1967 NBA Champion Philadelphia 76 Ers.* MacMillan Publishing, 2002

50. pghusa.blogspot.com/2007/07/first-flight-gustav-whitehead-schenley.html

51. Pittsburgh Post-Gazette, February 27, 1967

52. Pittsburgh Post-Gazette, March 31, 1967

53. Pittsburgh Post-Gazette, April 7, 1967

53. http://www.steelerettes.com/1966.htm

54. http://www.pittsburghhockey.net/HornetsPages/HornetsTIME1.html

54. Pittsburgh Post-Gazette, May 1, 1967 page 26

55. Pittsburgh Post-Gazette, June 9, 1967

56. http://user.pa.net/~ejjeff/timeline.html

56. http://www.razorandtiemedia.com/archives/2007/2007_06_01_2007_06_30.php

57. Pittsburgh Post-Gazette, July 15, 1967

57. Mary Brignano, *Pittsburgh Civic Light Opera: How The Dreams Came True,* Sewickley, PA, White Oak Publishing, 1996

58. Pittsburgh Post Gazette, August 30, 1967

58. http://www.liberace.org/liberace_biography/trivia.php

59. Liam Maguire, *What's The Score?* Random House Canada, 2001, p.97

60. Liam Maguire, What's The Score? Random House Canada, 2001, p.97

61. http://www.remembertheaba.com

61. Pittsburgh Post Gazette, October 25, 1967

62. Pittsburgh Post Gazette, December 10, 1967

1968

63. http://www.contrib.andrew.cmu.edu/usr/es36/history/dates.html

64. http://remembertheaba.com

65. http://www.pittsburghhockey.net/PensPages/Mascots/mascots.html

66. http://remembertheaba.com

67. http://www.piaa.org/champioships/archive/default.aspx

67. http://www.pahoops.org/records.htm

68. http://remembertheaba.com

68. http://www.nba.com/history/this_date_may.html

68. Observer-Reporter, Washington, PA, May 6, 1968

69. http://pittsburghhockey.net/PensPages/Mascots/mascots.html

69. en.wikipedia.org/wiki/Penguin_Pete

1969

70. www.RoundballClassic.net

71. Mary Brignano, *The Pittsburgh Civic Light Opera: How the Dreams Came True,* Sewickley PA, White Oak Publishing, 1996.

71. Pittsburgh Post-Gazette, July 23, 1969

72. www.post-gazette.com/pg/07021/755217-85stm

73. Pittsburgh Post-Gazette, December 2, 1969

74. http://www3.telus.net/Orr/timeline

74. Pittsburgh Post-Gazette, December 19, 1969

75. http://remembertheaba.com

1970

76. http://www.pittsburghlive.com/x/pittsburghtrib/s_77450.html

76. www.ledzeppelin.com/timeline/1970?page=1

77. http://www.contrib.andrew.cmu.edu/usr/es36/history/dates.html

78. http://www.thedoors.cz/brightmidnight.html

78. http://www.cd-bootleg.com/giras_doors.html

79. Pittsburgh Post-Gazette, October 11, 1970

79. http://pittsburghhockey.net/PensPages/Mascots/mascots.html

80. http://remembertheaba.com

81. http://remembertheaba.com

82. http://remembertheaba.com

83. pittsburghpanthers.cstv.com/sports/m-baskbl/spec-rel/pitt-centennial.html

83. http://espn.go.com/classic/biography/s/Wooden_John.html

Chapter 3, 1971-1975

1971

<u>83) February 13</u>

Everyone gets a chance to play today.

On this mid-winter Saturday afternoon the Civic Arena held three different hockey games from three different leagues. The action got started at noon when the Ramblers took on the Vikings in a Bantam League game. Then at 2:00pm the big boys took over. The Pittsburgh Penguins faced the talented Chicago Blackhawks in front of a crowd of 10,755. The Pens jumped out early bagging 4 goals in the first period. Leading the way was Syl Apps Jr. with 2 goals in a 20-second span. The Blackhawks eventually clawed their way back but fell short at the end. They lost the game 5-4. The Pens win, gave coach Red Kelly his 100th NHL victory.

After the game about 2000 fans stayed to watch what was recorded as the first collegiate hockey game played at the Civic Arena. This one featured Carnegie Mellon University Tartans (Pittsburgh) and the St. Vincent College Bearcats (Latrobe). At the start of the game, as the referee readied to drop the puck, St. Vincent seemed ill-prepared. One Bearcat defenseman was down on one knee re-lacing his skates while goalie Andy Labrasca was down saying a prayer. The trouble was Labrasca hadn't put on his mask, gloves nor goalie stick. As a result, just 8 seconds later, Carnegie Mellon had a 1- 0 lead. The Bearcats, fumbling from the beginning never quite got on tract. In fact later in the game one of their players, Gerry Hyner, was sent to the Mercy Hospital where he received 5 stitches courtesy of a high stick. Finally with only 15 seconds left in the contest, St. Vincent's, Bob Farrell got a breakaway but more disappointment arose. Farrell thought the final buzzer had sounded so he shot the puck into the corner. However, there was still 3 seconds left in the game! What he actually heard was an air horn from a celebrating Tartan fan. When the game ended soon after, the missed opportunity notwithstanding, didn't matter as the Bearcats were embarrassed 10-3.

Did you know that St. Vincent College has been the training camp for the Pittsburgh Steelers since 1967? Did you also know ex-president George Bush gave the commencement speech there on May 11, 2007?

84) March 6

Condor crashes record

In hoops action the Pittsburgh Condors outlasted the Floridians 142-129. Stew Johnson of the Condors went on a tear as he pumped in 62 points. At the time this set an individual ABA scoring record. Unfortunately less than a year later the record was broken. Zelmo Beaty of Utah scored 63 points when his Stars, ironically, beat Pittsburgh 149 to 140 in Salt Lake City on February 21, 1972 in front of 9,023 fans.

Did you know the previous ABA record for most points in a game was 59 and the Condors previous record was 57-set by Connie Hawkins?

85) March 26 & 27

The A, AA, and AAA finals all in one weekend

In the PIAA (Pennsylvania Inter-Scholastic Athletic Association) Basketball Championships, 7,097 people saw Mount Penn easily beat Laurel Valley 66-41 to capture the A final. Laurel Valley didn't help their cause when they missed 8 straight baskets to start the second half. As for Mt. Penn, this was their second state title. Their first one came at the Civic Arena in 1968 when they beat Williamsburg in a much tighter game 62 to 61.

As fans rested after the A final, some "cats" were ready to take to the hardwood for the AA Final. This one would feature the Midland Leopards and the Camp Hill Lions. As the game got underway, Midland pounced on Camp Hill taking a 14 to 0 lead. The Lions slowly got back into the game but never quite recovered. They would go on to lose 61-52. Camp Hill had won the state title in 1968 but couldn't duplicate it this time.

On March 27, The Schenley Spartans (Pittsburgh) entertained the Norristown Eagles for the prestigious AAA Final. This time a bigger crowd (8,288) came to cheer their local Spartans. However, the Eagles were ready and flew out to 7 to 4 lead. Schenley finally woke up and rattled off 11 consecutive points. From there the flood gates were opened. Led by Rick Coleman's 21 points the Spartans cruised to a 77 to 60 victory. By the way, Schenley had won their first state championships in 1966. Again it was held at the Civic Arena.

Did you know before the AA championships both Midland and Camp Hill had only 1 defeat each?

86) March 29

A plethora of punches!

On this night the Civic Arena hosted the Diamond Belt Boxing card. The 5,474 fans coming out witnessed 22 fights in both the open and novice divisions. One of the strangest matches in the open category saw Danny Kaminski take on Marshall Borowski in the 147-pound weight category. At one point the 2 boxers butted heads so severely that they both landed on the mat in a heap. After a short spell, Kaminski was the only one able to get back to his feet. He was declared the winner by knockout at 1:07 in the third round.

In another fight Bobby Romea stopped Chuck Coleman in the 108-pound category. Not to be outdone, Bobby's brother Rick won a decision over Richard Steigerwald in the 125-pound open division. The latter Romea was the 1970 champ but his match was no walk in the park. Steigerwald chased and pounded him throughout the first round. In the second Romea took control and continued so in the third round. The referees gave him the win on points.

Some of the winners this night went on to the National AAU championships in April of that year.

Did you know with three victories under their belt, the Shaeffer Boys' Club of Uniontown won the team championships for the evening?

87) July 12

"Holy cow" what a show!

Were you there when the KQV Summer Festival of Rock presented Jesus Christ Superstar-The Rock Opera? Pittsburgh was privileged to be the first stop on the tour of this production. On this night 13,000 Jesus freaks filled the Civic Arena.

Jesus Christ Superstar was originally a concept album released in 1970. The subsequent rock opera was the brain child of composer Andrew Lloyd Weber and lyricist Tim Rice. The show depicted the last week of Jesus Christ's life on earth. Though still popular to this day, the production was not without its detractors. Many Christians and Jews were offended by its controversial content.

Did you know Jesus Christ Superstar made its Broadway debut on October 12, 1971? A movie version also came out in 1973.

88) July 30

The future "King of Pop" makes his debut

Were you there when The Jackson 5 performed for the first time at the Civic Arena? Michael, who was only 12 years old, led older brothers Jackie, Tito, Jermaine and Marlon in an evening of singing and dancing. The opening act was the Commodores with none other than Lionel Ritchie.

The Jackson 5 would have a good year in 1971. They won a NAACP Image Award for the Best Singing Group of the Year and captured a Grammy Award for Best Pop Song with "ABC".

Did you know the Jackson 5 would perform at the Civic Arena two more times in their career? The first one was July 15, 1972 and the second one July 20, 1973. On July 15, 1974 they performed at Three Rivers Stadium.

89) October 10

A little inter-league history takes place

On this night the defending National Basketball Association (NBA) champs took on the Pittsburgh Condors of the American Basketball Association (ABA) in a pre-season exhibition game. This was historical as it marked the first and only time an NBA team played an ABA team at the Pittsburgh Civic Arena.

For the record, Milwaukee MVP Kareem Abdul-Jabbar did not play due to an eye injury. The 8,881 fans expecting to see the star were disappointed and booed when the announcement was made before the game. Kareem did show up for the contest but sat in his civvies.

As for the game itself, the Condors put up a good fight for two periods. In fact at half-time they had a 53-45 lead. In the third quarter Milwaukee slowly took over, especially their big men. Hall of fame point guard Oscar (Big O) Robertson led the charges as the Bucks found their scoring rhythm. By the fourth quarter they continued to steamroll over the Condors and cruised to a 129-115 victory. Robertson finished the night with a game-high 27 points and 10 assists. Teammate and fellow sensation Bob Dandridge, no slouch himself, pumped in 24 points. On the Condor side John Brisker was the high man with 24 while Stew Johnson chipped in 22.

Did you know what league rules the game was played under? The first half was played using NBA ones while the second half was played under ABA regulations.

90) December 27

School's Out?

As part of his "Killer" tour, Alice Cooper's freak show rolled into town. Kids on their Christmas break took advantage of their free time and packed the Igloo. In fact, at the time, the attendance of 14,400 set a rock concert record for the Civic Arena.

Cooper's repertoire of songs included: Under My Wheels, Halo of Flies, You Drive Me Nervous and I'm Eighteen. Opening acts were Bloodrock and the J. Giels Band.

Did you know Alice Cooper's real name was Vincent Damon Furnier? His grandfather, Thurman Sylvester Furnier, was an apostle in the Church of Jesus Christ based in Monongahela, Pennsylvania.

1972

91) February 18

A former champ is in the house!

On this night John Brisker scored 35 points as he led his Pittsburgh Condors to a 124-116 victory over the Memphis Pros. As an added bonus fans got a preliminary treat. Former heavyweight champ Mohammad Ali, weighing in at 227lbs., (about 20 pounds overweight) fought 10 exhibition boxing rounds against 4 separate opponents. One of them, heavyweight Dave Matthews (not the singer) was from Akron, Ohio. Matthews had a record of 18-1 and fought

Ali for 4 rounds. The other three boxers, "Ali" Miglioretti, Ben Harris and Sam McGill each had 2 rounds apiece. McGill, who was actually from the Pittsburgh area, put Ali down with a right hander. The ex-champ staggered to his corner at the end of the round.

Did you know the announced crowd of 6,400 looked only like 2,000? Ali wasn't to impressed either and commented "Pittsburgh is a hick city."

92) March 11

A great one reaches a milestone

The hometown Pittsburgh Penguins outlasted the Boston Bruins 6-4 this evening but accolades went to someone from the losing team. Bruin star defenseman Bobby Orr scored once and collected 2 assists. His goal would be his 500th career point-in just 396 games!

Did you know what happened the day after this game? The same two teams met in Boston and Penguin Darryl Edestrand scored twice in 9 seconds. The goals came in the third period and helped erase a 3-goal deficit. Pittsburgh would manage a 4-4 tie with the Bruins.

Though Boston couldn't beat Pittsburgh in these 2 games they did go on to capture another Stanley Cup this season. Bobby Orr would again lead the way as he would win the Conn Smythe, Hart Memorial and the James Norris trophies. He also was the NHL Plus/Minus award winner.

93) July 22

A rolling stone gathers no moss.

The evening started when Stevie Wonder warmed up the audience with his band Wonderlove. Then the sold-out crowd got hit with the Rolling Stones. Mick Jagger led the way as he jumped and gyrated like a juiced up energizer bunny. Wearing a form-fitting purple jumpsuit, Jagger commanded the stage at every move. On the song "Midnight Rambler" he got down on the stage and started to whip an invisible victim with a sash. Later on, while prancing around, a glass object thrown from the audience came dangerously close to hitting him. Jagger quickly retorted "Don't go throwing your bottles up here at me!"-at which the house violently cheered.

While folks inside the Civic Arena were enjoying the Stones, the scene outside was quite different. People who had not gotten tickets started their own party but it went too far. The police ended up arresting 60 people for disorderly conduct or intoxication.

Did you know the Rolling Stones had 30 new speakers at their show? Their old ones were damaged in an explosion on July 17th in Montreal. The blast happened in front of the Montreal Forum and it was so severe it blew out windows from across the street.

94) November 22

The Penguins save the best for the last period

Were you there when the Pittsburgh Penguins defeated the St. Louis Blues 10-4? The Penguins scored 7 times in the third period alone! Of the 7 goals, 5 were scored in a span of 2 minutes and 7 seconds-an NHL record. The 5 scorers were Bryan Hextall on a power play goal at the 12:00 minute mark, Jean Pronovost at 12:18, Al McDonough at 13:40, Ken Schinkel at 13:49 and Ron Schock at 14:07. By the way Al McDonough had a hat trick that night.

Did you know the Penguins still hold the NHL record for the 5 fastest goals by a team?

1973

95) February 23

That's a lot of beef

As part of a wrestling bill, 10, 321 fans were treated to the Texas Death Match-no holds barred. Local favorite Bruno "The Italian Superman" Sammartino took on Prof. Toru Tanaka in this highly anticipated match.

Earlier that year (Jan.19) Prof. Toru Tanaka used the ropes to defeat Sammartino. Two weeks later (Feb. 2) Sammartino got his revenge in a vicious battle in which both men were bloodied. With the series even at 1-1 the stage was set on this day for the tie-breaker. Sammartino used the hometown crowd to his advantage and sealed victory in the Texas Death Match.

On this day the crowd also witnessed 2 tag team matches. In one of them, "Killer" Kowalski and his partner-fan favorite George "The Animal" Steele beat Tony Parisi and Dom DeNucci. In the other match, Blackjack Mulligan and Blackjack Lanza took care of Frank Holtz and Larry Zbryszko.

Some highlights of the individual matches were: a victory for The Executioner, a disqualification for Eric The Red and fighting ejections for both Waldo Von Erich and Baron Scicluna.

Did you know Prof. Toru Tanaka passed away in August, 2000 of heart failure? In 2008 Sammartino turned 72 years old.

96) June 19

"I think I can see the moon man!"

The Pink Floyd concert hits the 'Burgh. This was the first and only time that the British mega-group played at the Civic Arena. The band had played concerts in Pittsburgh before and even after this date but they were at other venues.

One of the highlights of the evening came when the boys were playing "Dark Side of the Moon". As if on cue, the retractable roof opened up to the awe of the audience. A cloud of smoke rising from the floor to the open sky enthralled everyone. Some say the stuff in the air was dry ice while others claim it was the burning effects from all the funny tobacco. This author reserves judgment.

Did you know this concert was delayed 2 hours because the band had an airline problem?

97) June 25 + 26

The King finally arrives after all these years.

Elvis Presley made his first ever appearances at the Pittsburgh Civic Arena on these dates. On the first night he drew 14,335 fans while on the second night it was 14,296. At the time they were attendance records.

Some of the songs Elvis played that night were: I'm Leavin, How Great Thou Art, Help Me Make It ThroughThe Night, What Now My Love and I'll Remember You.

98) September 22

Liza leaves them wanting more

On this night the daughter of Judy Garland did her mother proud. Liza Minnelli gave a thrilling show filled with song, dance and personality. The 27-year old Academy Award winner (1972) didn't rest on her laurels as she gave a well choreographed performance. Her strong vocals grabbed the audience and kept them attentive all night. Whether performing show tunes or ballads sitting on a stool, the crowd was simply mesmerized. The energetic Minnelli kept things moving with dazzling dance steps that showed her polished theatrical background. Pleased with her strength and agility the 6, 825 in attendance rewarded her with standing ovations. Minnelli performed for 90 minutes while never taking a break. In her final encore she showed the depth of her voice with a powerful rendition of Cabaret. The song which made her famous, started out fast and bold. The second verse quieted as Minnelli described her girlfriend Elsie who lived in Chelsea. As the final chorus started Liza raised her voice once more as the orchestra hit a powerful crescendo. Just then the lights turned on as energy busted through the air. With the show dramatically over the crowd jumped to their feet for a final standing ovation.

Did you know entertainment writer George Anderson of the Pittsburgh Post-Gazette was very impressed by Liza Minnelli? He stated "…it was the best show I've ever seen at the Civic Arena…"

1974

99) January 23

These new Penguins are rough around the edges

On this night the Pittsburgh Penguins faced the St. Louis Blues. There was a buzz in the Civic Arena air as newly acquired Penguin tough guys Bob "Battleship" Kelly and Steve "Mental Case" Durbano (who both arrived from St. Louis) made their debuts. The Penguins needed a little more grit in their game and the two new lads didn't disappoint. Both players threw their bodies around hitting everything in sight. In the second period alone things got so rough the referees called 50 minutes of penalties. Durbano was in the middle of it all with his first fight as a Pen.

On the scoreboard, Pittsburgh beat St. Louis 4 to 1 as the biggest crowd ever to witness a hockey game at the Igloo cheered on. The attendance was 13,324. Both Kelly and Durbano were impressive in their first starts and were named co-first stars of the game. This was significant as it marked the first time in Penguin history that 2 players shared this honor.

Did you know Steve Durbano's other nickname was "Demolition Durby?"

100) March 31

A great play by a great player

In a nail-biter, Team U.S defeated Team Pennsylvania 77-76 in the tenth annual Dapper Dan Roundball Classic. Lanky Moses Malone made a steal then scored (slam dunk) with 9 seconds left in the basketball game to give Team U.S. the close victory. Malone ended the night with 31 points and 20 rebounds.

Did you know the 6'11" Moses Malone was the top rank schoolboy in the nation this year?

101) July 26

A music triple play

Fans coming to the Civic Arena heard sweet sounds and melodies all evening. Linda Ronstadt started things off with such songs as Silver Threads and Golden Needles, Break My Mind, Your No Good, and Buddy Holly's That'll Be the Day. She also threw in some ballads like Colorado, Desperado and Love Has No Pride. Reports indicate her voice was in fine form as she breezed through her eclectic song selection. The roof was opened about one-fourth of the way on this summer night. Arena officials didn't want to open it more since skies were slightly overcast.

After the nice warm up, fans got to hear the harmonies of America. Dewey Bunnell led the group with such hits as I Need You, Tin Man, Lonely People, Sand Man, and Ventura Highway. Gerry Beckley tickled the ivory on one set of songs that garnished him a standing ovation. The show ended with a couple encores including A Horse With No Name.

The last performer of the night was James Taylor. With everyone in a warm fuzzy mood and the threat of rain gone the roof was fully opened. Taylor came out as casual as his attire-he seemed to be wearing white "pajamas". Again he was at the top of his game and belted out songs such as: I'm a Night Owl, Honey, Me and My Guitar, One-Man Parade and Rock 'n' Roll is Music Now. His voice smooth as silk carried off ballads and hits effortlessly. They included Carolina in My Mind, Don't Let Me be Lonely Tonight, Sweet Baby James and Fire and Rain.

Overall, fans got one of the best combination concerts ever at the Civic Arena. The singing and music blended superbly. In addition, seems no one went home with a broken ear drum.

102) August 14

Some new faces from the Great White North

On this night Uriah Heep and Manfred Mann performed at the Civic Arena. There were two opening acts, Earth Band and a little known three-man group from Canada. The Canadian artists would eventually become one of the most popular bands in the world. Their name was Rush.

This was a special occasion for Rush as it was their first concert on their first American tour. Ironically, drummer Neil Peart had only joined the band two weeks before this, on July 29. Though Rush had played individual dates in the U.S. before this time, (i.e. in Michigan) they had never toured the U.S. nor was Peart part of the band. The attendance for the concert that night was slightly over 11,000.

103) December 6

The new Lady Panthers start with a bang!

In the first game played by the Pittsburgh Panthers women's basketball team (modern era) they hammered their cross city rivals Duquesne Dukes 91 to 32.

1975

104) March 8

The Penguins blast the Broad Street Bullies

Were you there when Pittsburgh Penguins man-handled the Philadelphia Flyers 8-2? During this sold-out game, Penguins defenseman Ron Stackhouse tied 2 NHL records in one game. The first, getting 4 assists in one period for a defenseman and the second, getting 6 assists in one game for a defenseman. Up to this date only 3 other defensemen had 6 assists in a game. They were Babe Pratt, Pat Stapleton and Bobby Orr.

Did you know since Stackhouse's record tying game two other defensemen have collected 6 assists in one game? They were Paul Coffey and Gary Suter.

105) April 6

The boys hit the mats!

This was the date of the First Annual Pittsburgh Press Old Newsboys Wrestling Classic (now called Dapper Dan Wrestling Classic). In all, 12 matches pitting Team USA against Team Pennsylvania were contested. One of the highlights included George Kavacas (Lowell, Mass.) against Angelo Marino in the 105-pound category. Kavacas had a perfect 28-0 record for the season while Marino hadn't lost in 59 tries. The match started tight and stayed that way until the end. With less than a minute to go, Kavacas had a narrow 3 to 2 lead. Marino, desperate to tie the match tried 2 takedowns with 30 and 15 seconds left. Kavacas stood his ground and hung on for the slim victory. Marino, dejected would lose for the first time in more than 2 years.

In another close match Frank DeAngelis (N.Y.) beat PIAA champ John Eichenlaub 8 to 6 in the138-pound category. Eichenlaub had a 29-0 record before losing that night. Pennsylvania did have some bright spots. Billy Bertrand whipped Shawn Whitcomb (Grand Rapids, Mich.) 16 to 1 in the 185-pound category. For Bertrand this was his 80th win in three years. Also Steve Maurey beat Brian Evans (Norman, Oklahoma) 10 to 3 in the 126-pound weight. There was some irony in this match because back in 1951, Evans' father had beaten Maurey's father in an NCAA tournament. Talk about sweet revenge!

By the end of the night Team USA was too much for Team Pennsylvania and won the inaugural Wrestling Classic. The final score was 30 to 13. Other Pennsylvania wrestlers that night were: Mark Richard, Dan Perri, Shawn Griffith, Mike Gill, R. McIntyre, Bill Amelio, Jan Hockenbroch and Bob Bickellman.

Did you know on the same day WPIAL defeated Maryland 34-9 in preliminary wrestling matches? The attendance was 6,784.

106) April 26

The Pens fall from grace

On this evening the Pittsburgh Penguins hosted the New York Islanders in play-off action. The second round series was tied 3 games to 3 and a victory by the Pens would put them into the Conference Final. A Pens loss however, would not only end their season but put them in some dubious company. Pittsburgh would become only the second team in NHL play-off history to have blown a 3 game to 0 lead. The last time it happened was to the Detroit Red Wings in 1942. They were leading the Toronto Maple Leafs 3 games to 0 in the Stanley Cup Finals but then lost the next 4 in a row.

The Isles and Pens started this game very defensively. The tight checking affair would carry over to the third period. With still no score late into the game, the Isles finally got a break. Their 34 year-old captain, Ed Westfall scored at the 5:18 mark to give them the lead. The Pens desperately tried to get the equalizer but Islander goalie Chico Resch stood tall. Even in the last minute as the Pens put 6 attackers on the ice Resch shut the door. The Islander victory and especially how they did would be a bitter pill to swallow for Pens fans for many years to come.

Did you know Syl Apps Sr. was on the Toronto Maple Leaf team that came back from a 3 to 0 deficit to win the Stanley Cup in 1942 while son Syl Apps Jr. was on the Penguin team that lost to the Islanders in the same fashion?

107) July 26

Game, set (record), match!

The Pittsburgh Triangles of the World Team Tennis (WTT) league defeated the N.Y.Sets 26-19 in team tennis action. The WTT was a co-ed league that featured some of the best players in the world (i.e. Jimmy Conners, Ile Nastase, Chris Everet etc.) On this special night the largest crowd ever to witness a tennis match in the Greater Pittsburgh area came to the Civic Arena. A total of 10,236 people saw some grueling tennis played by top notch players. Highlights included: Vitas Gerulaitis (Team Pittsburgh) beating his Wimbledon partner Sandy Mayer 6 to 4, Yvonne Goolagong (Team Pittsburgh) taking care of Billie Jean King by the same score and Goolagong and Peggy Michel (Team Pittsburgh) whipping King and Mona Schallau 6 to 2 in doubles match. The Triangles also set a league record by winning their 11th straight match.

Did you know the World Team Tennis league was started in 1974 and was co-founded by Billie Jean King?

108) August 24

On the verge of greatness

The Pittsburgh Triangles (WTT) tennis team hosted the San Francisco Golden Gaters in the second day of the Finals matches. Both teams were evenly matched with Pittsburgh having won the East division while San Francisco ruled the West. The best out of three series was 1 to 0 for San Francisco so Pittsburgh needed a victory just to stay alive. Though the attendance was only 2,182 the Triangles gave it all in their 5 matches. By the end of the day they had won 3, tied 1 and lost 1. They had beaten The Golden Gaters by a combined score of 28 to 25 to square the series 1-1. The Triangles didn't have much time to savor the victory because the next day the same two teams would meet in the rubber match. The winner this time would be crowned the 1975 champs.

Did you know Vitas Gerulaitus who was member of the Pittsburgh Triangles was once engaged to actress Janet Jones (now Mrs. Wayne Gretzky) for 3 years?

109) August 25

Triangles triumph!

The Pittsburgh Triangles defeated the San Francisco Golden Gaters 21-14 (and three day totals 74-65) in front of 6,882 jubilant spectators to capture the Bancroft Cup.

The Triangles were so dominant and had so many points that the Mixed Doubles portion didn't have to be played.

The nationally televised event was a great boost for the city of Pittsburgh and the sport of tennis. Fans at the match gave the Triangles a standing ovation in appreciation of their great year.

Did you know Triangle player Vitas Gerulaitis was named the playoff MVP?

110) December 29

Hot "Soviet Wings" burn the Penguins

The Soviet Wings took on the Pittsburgh Penguins in front of 13,218 curious fans. This was historical as it marked the first time club teams from the Russian elite hockey league challenged club teams from the National Hockey League. The Soviet Wing team had some additional help being bolstered by 3 of the best players from rival Spartak. One of these players Alexandr Yakushev was familiar to North American style hockey as he had played for Team Russia in the famous 8-game Summit Series against Team Canada in 1972.

On this particular night the Wings were flying. They stunned and awed Penguin fans by jumping out to a 5-0 lead on their brilliant skating and pin point passing. The Penguins made adjustments in the second period by fore checking more vigorously. It worked to a point as they slowly chipped away at the large deficit. However, it was not enough on this night. As the third period buzzer sounded the Wings flew away with a 7-4 victory.

Did you know Penguin forward Vic Hadfield also played in the Summit Series in 1972? His Canadian team barely won with 4 wins, 3 losses and 1 tie.

1971

83. Pittsburgh Post-Gazette, February 15, 1971

83. http://www.svchockey.com/history/highlights/1970-71.htm

84. http://remembertheaba.com

85. http://www.piaa.org/championships/archive/default.aspx

86. Pittsburgh Post-Gazette, March 30, 1971

87. http://user.pa.net/~ejjeff/timeline.htm

87. www.timrice.co.uk/jest.html

87. www.timrice.co.uk/jest.html

88. www.jackson5abc.com/dossiers/concerts

88. Lisa D. Campbell. *Michael Jackson: King of Pop*, Branden Books, 1993

89. http://remembertheaba.com

90. http://en.wikipedia.org/wiki/Alice_Cooper

90. http://en.wikipedia.org/wiki/Mellon_Arena

1972

91. http://remembertheaba.com

91. Observer-Reporter, Washington, PA, February 18 &19, 1972

92. Pittsburgh Post-Gazette, March 13, 1972

93. Pittsburgh Post-Gazette, July 23, 1972

94. http://letsgopens.com/penshist.htm

94. http://www.post-gazette.com/pg/07021/755217-85.stm

1973

95. Pittsburgh Post-Gazette, February 24, 1973

95. http://www.steelbeltwrestling.com/index.php?option=com_content&task=view&id=1208 Itemid=44

96. www.allfloyd.com/concerts/Past_Tours.html

96. http://www.post-gazette.com/pg/07021/755217-85sm

97. http?/www.elvis-in-concert.com/

98. Pittsburgh Post Gazette, September 25, 1973

1974

99. Joe Starkey, *Tales from the Pittsburgh Penguins*, Champaign, IL, Sports Publishing LLC, 2006

99. stlouisblueslegends.blogspot.com

100. http://www.pahoops.org.gyms.htm

101. Pittsburgh Press, July 27, 1974

102. http://en.wikipedia.org/wiki/Rush_(band)

102. http://www.cygnus=x1.net/links/rush/tourdates.php

103. Pittsburgh Post-Gazette, December 5, 1974

1975

104. http://members.tripod.com/~broadstreetcrib/nhlrec.htm

104. http://letsgopens.com/penshist.htm

105. http://www.wrestlingclassic.com/2007/news

105. http://www.post-gazette.com/pg/07084/771694-364.stm

106. http://espn.go.com/page2/s/list/chokes/hockey.html

106. Pittsburgh Post-Gazette, April 27, 1975

107. Pittsburgh Post-Gazette, July 28, 1975 page 22.

108. Pittsburgh Post-Gazette, August 25, 1975

109. http://www3.telerama.com/~johnv/tennis/wtt5.htm

110. http://www.1972summitseries.com/ssgame2.html

110. Pittsburgh Post Gazette, December 30, 1975

Chapter 4, 1976-1980

1976

111) January 23

The two best are kicked out

In wrestling action at the Igloo, Pittsburgh fans got to see big bruisers, tiny tikes and everything in between. Some of the characters involved were: 6'5"-400lb Gorilla Monsoon taking on Baron Mikel Scicluna (originally from the Isle of Malta), midgets Jamaca Kid and Dirty Morgan teamed up against Little Louie and Sonny Boy Hayes while Dr. Bill Miller (a real veterinarian) clashed with "Pistol" Pete Sanchez.

In the main event World Wide Wrestling Federation Champion and Pittsburgh local Bruno Sammartino fought Superstar Billy Graham. Unfortunately there was no winner this night but also no loser. Both bad boys got eliminated in a double disqualification. The attendance that night was 7,000.

Did you know Superstar Billy Graham's real name is Eldridge Wayne Coleman? Coleman took on the ring name Billy Graham as a tribute to the famous evangelist after being converted to Christianity at a revival meeting. He added the Superstar part after hearing the song Jesus Christ Superstar.

112) March 24

Two Penguins get team records on the same day

Late in the hockey season the Pittsburgh Penguins tied the Boston Bruins 5-5. Popular Pittsburgh forward Jean Pronovost scored his 50th goal of the season and in the process became the first Penguin ever to reach this milestone. In the same game Penguin forward Pierre Larouche collected his 100th point of the season. Again this was a milestone in Penguin history.

Did you know a couple weeks after this game Larouche also got his 50th goal of the season?

113) April 4

The Cowboys get a little revenge

Were you there when the Dallas Cowboys defeated the Pittsburgh Steelers 81 to 73? Was this a football game? No it was a charity basketball played by the two teams. Money raised went to benefit the Muscular Dystrophy Foundation. The crowd of 8,479 was one of the largest ever to witness the Steelers basketball team.

In the contest, Too Tall Jones (Cowboys) and Ernie Holmes (Steelers) took turns crashing the boards for their respective teams. Holmes, a fan favorite that day, also physically crashed into a couple of Cowboys. One was Mitch Hoopes and the other Bill Gregory-the later rocking the Civic Arena all over. Furthermore, on one play, Holmes dribbled the ball the length of the court while taking out former teammate Preston Pearson en route. Though he was a presence on the hardwood, it was teammate John Stallworth finishing as the top Steeler scorer with 15 points.

Did you know 2 and half months before this game the Pittsburgh Steelers defeated the Dallas Cowboys 21 to 17 in Superbowl X?

114) October 20

A diamond is a girl's best friend.

Were you there among the 13,749 fans at the Neil Diamond concert? The show started 40 minutes late but Diamond made up for lost time with a spectacular entrance. What seemed like a sacred moment, the music and choir built to a hymn-like climax. Diamond stood in the dim glow at center stage with hands clasped and head bowed. As the drums rolled and the lights brightened Diamond turned to the hungry crowd, raised his arms and belted out the words to "Sooolaimon". Two and a half hours and 3 encores later, Diamond had the audience begging for more-except the few who had earlier passed out!

115) December 14

Don't blink you might miss something!

The Chinese Acrobats of Taiwan took the Civic Arena by storm. In their U.S. debut tour, 65 performers and musicians dazzled audiences with super human acts of levitation, Kung Fu, ribbon dances, tumbling and juggling, feats of balance on rolling bicycles, chairs and tables and breathtaking aerial displays.

116) December 31

Pittsburgh celebrates the New Year with a special guest

More than 16,400 Pittsburgh fans rang in the New Year with the "King"-Elvis Presley. However, long before he appeared, three opening acts that included the Sweet Inspirations and the Stamps Quartet entertained the festive crowd. With anticipation building after a long intermission, Elvis finally appeared at 11:25 pm. Fans went hysterical as screams and flashbulbs went off in all directions. The "King" played for 90 minutes and had the crowd begging for more. At one moment close to midnight he told the crowd, "I would like to wish you all a happy and prosperous New Year, and health and happiness throughout 1977." He then sang "Funny How Time Slips Away" followed by "Auld Lang Syne" As usual some lucky fans got a piece of Elvis when he threw out towels (42 in all signifying his upcoming 42nd birthday on January 8) of sweat all night. Some claim Elvis was in top form this night interacting with the crowd and taking audience requests. Later in the show Presley introduced his father Vernon and daughter Lisa Marie.

Unfortunately this would be the last concert the "King" would play at the Pittsburgh Civic Arena. Presley died August 17, 1977 at the age of 42.

Did you know that this concert is available on CD? It is called Elvis: New Years Eve (1976 FTD 2CD).

1977

117) May 7

Borg versus Borsch

The Soviet National tennis team of the World Team Tennis league defeated Cleveland-Pittsburgh Nets 25-23. The Soviet team, who had stars like Alex Metreveli and Olga Morozova played only one year in the league and at one point, was called the Pennsylvania Keystones. They were also the first foreign national team to play regularly in an American sports league. The Cleveland team, on the other hand, had poor attendance in 1977 so they played half their home games in cities like Pittsburgh, Nashville, Miami and New Orleans. Their premier player was the great Bjorn Borg. This was his first year in the league and by years' end Borg captured both the Male Rookie of the Year award and Male All-Star Game MVP.

Did you know only 600 people showed up for this tennis match?

118) August 7

The NBA takes on some of Pittsburgh's best

Were you there for the first Annual Summer Pro Basketball Classic? The event attracted 10,404 fans wanting to see past and present heroes from the hardwood.

The game was dominated by offense as the NBA Stars defeated the Pittsburgh Local Stars 138-136 in double overtime. Fans saw a lot of scoring but the play was slow and sloppy. Players not in mid-season form dribbled terribly and made bad passes all night. The best of the lot was Calvin Murphy. He had 25 points for the victors and was named the game's MVP.

Former Schenley High stars Maurice Lucas (Portland Trail Blazers) and Ken Durrett played for the Local Stars. Lucas led all scorers with 27 points and 15 rebounds. Former Duquesne grad Mike Barr (Kansas City Kings) also played for the "home team". At the beginning of the game fans gave a warm welcome and standing ovation to past Pittsburgh Piper and Ren star Connie Hawkins. The 34 year-old ABA champ (1967-68) pitched in 13 for the Pittsburgh Locals. Former Piper teammate Tom Washington finished the night with 9 points.

119) September 10

Color me country!

On this night the Igloo was warmed up by The Grand Ole Opry On Tour. Country fans were treated to 2 shows and got to see legends such as: Roy Acuff, Grandpa Jones, Ernest Tubb, Hank Snow, Don Gibson, Bob Luman, Jeannie Selly, Minnie Pearl, Jack Greene, Del Reeves, The Osborne Brothers, The Wilburn Brothers, Charlie Louvin and Debbie Groves. If this wasn't enough talent all ready, special guests included: Billy Jo Spears, Benny Dean and Shades of Blue and the Ralph Case Cloggers.

Did you know Hank Snow who died in 1999 is in the: Nashville Songwriters Hall of Fame, Country Music Hall of Fame, Canadian Music Hall of Fame, the Nova Scotia Music Hall of Fame and the Canadian Country Music Hall of Fame?

1978

120) August 1-2, 4, 8, 11-12, 14-17

Something fishy is going on here

Parts of the movie 'The Fish That Saved Pittsburgh' were shot at the Civic Arena on these days. More specifically, the stars of the film were the laughable last place Pittsburgh Pythons, a mock NBA team. During the movie the Pythons soon became the Pittsburgh Pisces (thus the fish connotation) after consulting an astrologist Mona Mondieu (Stockard Channing) for advice on improving their dismal record. Eventually the Pisces turned their season around and made it all the way to the league championships. In the final game they hosted the powerful Los Angeles Lakers. The Lakers lineup boasted some real pros that included: Kareem Abdul-Jabbar, Ron Carter Jr., Lou Hudson, Norm Nixon (former Duquesne stand out) and Connie Hawkins (former Pittsburgh Ren and Piper). The star player for the Pisces was Julius "Dr. J" Erving. Other notable personalities in the film included: Jonathan Winters, Stockard Channing, Meadowlark Lemon, Flip Wilson, James Bond III, Debbie Allen and Marv Albert.

If you saw the film you may recall how the Pisces made their entrance for the final game. They came in a hot air balloon through the retractable roof of the Civic Arena.

Over the years, this wacky basketball flick has become somewhat of a cult classic. It had a little bit of everything including: funky music, afros, good and bad acting, comedy, sports, a psychedelic basketball court and a disco atmosphere.

Did you know in 1984 Norm Nixon married actress Debbie Allen?

121) October 7

A couple famous hoopsters pay a visit

On this evening the Philadelphia 76'ers featuring Julius "Dr. J" Erving took on the New Orleans Jazz who had "Pistol" Pete Maravich (Aliquippa). The NBA exhibition game was supposed to highlight two of the best stars in the league. Unfortunately, a day before the showdown Maravich left town with an apparent back problem. Despite the disappointment, the hometown crowd of 10,651 saw a great game and a couple other great stars. The 76'ers led by 6'11" 275-pounder Darryl "Chocolate Thunder" Dawkins destroyed New Orleans 109-84. Dawkins had a team high 17 points but impressed fans most with 4 slam dunks, 2 of which collapsed the rim. Not far behind was 6'11" teammate Caldwell Jones who had 16 points. Erving had 9 points in 21 minutes of play but had fans "awing" with his slick moves and passing prowess.

Did you know Pete Maravich died of a heart attack at the age of 40 on January 5, 1988 after playing a pickup basketball game in Pasadena, California? His last words, spoken to fellow player and Focus on the Family head James Dobson, were: I need to do this more often. I'm really feeling good."

122) December 28

Fans get a kick out of Pittsburgh's new team

Were you there when the Pittsburgh Spirit played their first regular season game as members of the Major Indoor Soccer League (MISL)? Almost 6,000 fans came out to see them take on the mighty New York Arrows. Pittsburgh played an entertaining game but couldn't contain Arrow superstar Steve Zungul. Zungul finished the night with 2 goals and 2 assists as his New York team doubled the score on the Spirit 6-3.

Did you know Steve Zungul was later suspended by the U.S. Soccer Federation because of conflicting contracts with the New York Arrows and the Yugoslav National team?

1979

123) February 2

My 'Spirit' takes a kicking!

On this mid winter night in Pittsburgh, Civic Arena spectators got a taste of international soccer. In a special exhibition game, the Moscow Spartak soccer club manhandled the Pittsburgh Spirit 8-2. The 5,832 startled fans saw how the Russians led by Georgij Jartsev dominated play with slick passing and precise ball control. Their team had great chemistry and it showed against the new and inexperienced Spirit. Pittsburgh's only goal scorers for the night were Dave Hoffmeyer and John Dorinsky.

This exhibition game was the first in a series played by the visiting Russian squad against each club team in the new Major Indoor Soccer League (MISL). In their six-game tour Spartak accumulated a record of 5-1 and outscored their opponents 60-25. Their only defeat, 7-5, came at the hands of the MISL regular season winners the Houston Summit. The Summit boasted a veteran team led by Finnish star Kai Haaskivi.

Did you know most of the players on the Moscow Spartak team were students enrolled in Moscow's Physical Culture Institute?

124) March 23-24

The boys and girls show off their stuff

This was the first time that the Civic Arena held all the final games for the boys and girls PIAA Basketball Championships. The results were the following. For the girls, York Catholic defeated Johnsonburg 51-41 in the A final, Susquehanna Twp. beat Brentwood 64-52 in the AA final while Franklin Regional easily handled Lancaster McCaskey 68-42 in the AAA final. Franklin Regional's victory represented the first time in 12 years a school from the West (Pennsylvania) won the title. Cheryl Ellison led their squad with 33 points and 17 rebounds while teammate Pam Mihlasevich chipped in 22 points and 13 rebounds.

On the boys side, St. Pius X defeated Conemaugh 57-52 to win the A final. Conemaugh had entered the contest with a 30-game winning streak but couldn't keep their unblemished record. However, as consolation, star player Jeff Hostetler would go to have a great career as an NFL quarterback. A highlight came in 1991when he led the New York Giants to a 20-19 Super Bowl victory against the Buffalo Bills.

In the AA final York Catholic took care of Ford City 69-48 for their second straight title. Their victory, along with their female counterparts, gave York Catholic the distinction as being the first school in state history to capture the boys and girls titles in the same year.

Local school Allegheny-Kiski Valley disposed of William Allen 72-66 in the AAA final.

They were led by Varner with 28 points and 11 rebounds while teammate Pryor had 22 points. The attendance for the game was 7,022.

125) September 4-5

Night Fever overtakes the Civic Arena crowd

On these two nights over 34,000 packed the Civic Arena to see one of the hottest groups in the late 1970's-The Bee Gees. At the time, their 2 shows brought in the highest gross to date of the Igloo-$450,000.

Before the Gibb brothers hit the stage Sweet Inspirations warmed the audience playing such hits as: Hot Stuff, Knock On Wood, and I Will Survive. When the Bee Gees appeared they bombarded fans with 300 chrome lights, 40 speakers, a laser system and a great band.

Based on concerts reports, seems Barry and Robin's falsetto voices were in fine form. Meanwhile Maurice provided outstanding support to his brothers. The group played a lot of their hits like: I Started a Joke, Massachusetts, Tragedy, How Can You Mend a Broken Heart, Words and Run to Me. Some of their bigger songs, for example, Night Fever and Stayin' Alive came from the recently released and popular Saturday Night Fever LP. At the time the record was the biggest seller in the history of the recording industry with 23 million copies. Later Michael Jackson's Thriller would surpass this mark.

In all, it seems Bee Gee fans left the Civic "Disco" very happy.

Did you know a few years before these shows the Bee Gees drew one of the smallest crowds to the Civic Arena?

126) December 2

Who was to blame?

On this night The Who rocked the 'Burgh. The standing room only crowd heard the likes of My Generation, Won't Get Fooled Again and Who Are You. In a strange moment, while performing Behind Blue Eyes, firecrackers from the upper level were thrown on stage. When seeing them Pete Townsend retorted "If you see someone with a firecracker, kill him." He also said he would leave if it didn't stop. Though this was a rather minor incident it foreshadowed a worse thing to come. The next day (December 3rd) before a Who concert in Cincinnati a human stampede ensued resulting in terrible consequences. Eleven people were killed and many were injured as fans rushed to get into the stadium. To date the incident remains the worst tragedy in U.S. rock concert history.

Did you know the Who concert in Pittsburgh was described by one Post-Gazette writer as the best rock'n'roll concert in Pittsburgh in 1979 despite some sound problems?

1980

127) January 30

The Black and Gold turns a bit blue

In NHL action the St. Louis Blues visited the Pittsburgh Penguins. This was a unique night as it marked the first game in franchise history the Penguins wore their new black and gold uniforms. In the 1970's their city counterparts the Steelers and Pirates wore these colors and won six championships combined. The Penguins were hoping to capitalize on their luck.

In the game itself, the Penguins went into the third period trailing 4-3. They desperately wanted to tie the game and fired 18 shots at Blues goalie Mike Liut. Liut practically stood on his head as he stopped every blast. The Pens lost and the capacity crowd of 12,345 left feeling frustrated and a bit unlucky.

128) June 20

This ain't a sugar coated affair!

Roberto "manos de piedras" (Hands of Stone) Duran captured the World Boxing Council welterweight title when he defeated Sugar Ray Leonard in a

15-round unanimous decision in Montreal, Canada. The bout, fought at the Olympic Stadium was shown on closed-circuit television at the Civic Arena. The 12, 450 fans in attendance enjoyed one of the best scraps in boxing history. For the record, this was the first sold-out closed circuit event at the Civic Arena. It was so popular scalpers outside the arena were making a killing.

If you were at the Igloo that night you might remember some of the interesting under-card matches also. In one fight Sugar Ray's older brother Roger won a split decision over former middleweight Canadian Champion Clyde Gray. In another tilt Canadian heavyweight champ Trevor Berbick knocked out John Tate (former WBA heavyweight champ) in the 9th round. Meanwhile in the lightweight division Canadian champ Gaetan Hart knocked out Cleveland Denny. Denny was injured so badly he had to be taken to the hospital.

Meanwhile back at the main event, the 24-year old Sugar Ray Leonard suffered his first professional defeat. His tactic of trying to exchange blows with Duran backfired. Duran was able to withstand the pressure and deliver some good licks himself. The 29 year-old Panamanian would capture the title and raise his record to an astounding 70 wins and 1 loss. For Leonard, the setback was tough yet there were a couple consolation prizes. First, he became the first boxer in history to receive 10 million dollars for one fight and second, he would later win a rematch.

Did you know Sugar Ray Leonard was actually born Ray Charles Leonard after the famous singer.

129) December 13

Penguin player skates into record book

On this night the Philadelphia Flyers took on the Pittsburgh Penguins in another Battle of Pennsylvania. With a victory the Flyers would assume first place in the NHL standings. The Penguins had other ideas and came out flying. The Flyers, trying to keep up, took a rash of penalties to slow their opponents down. It proved costly and by mid game the Pens were up 5-2. Paul Baxter the 24-year old Pen centerman had done most of the damage. He popped in 4 goals and in the process put himself in the team record books. It was the first time any Penguin had scored 4 goals in a game. Three of his goals were scored on the power play and two came with Philly 2 men short.

With the Pens in a comfortable lead the outcome looked favorable for the hometown fans. Suddenly Philly woke up and narrowed the gap 5-3. Then pesky forward Bobby Clarke added 2 more goals (one short-handed) at the end of the second period and just like that the score was even at 5. With the momentum on their side the Flyers scored another one in the third frame. The Pens reeling, desperately tried to get the equalizer. With time running out they pulled their goalie in favor of an extra attacker. It was to no avail. The game ended 6-5 for Philly. For Pittsburgh their historical night finished on a sour note. The 12,165 fans did give Paul Baxter a standing ovation for his accomplishment but it was bittersweet.

1976

111. http://www.steelbeltwrestling.com/index.php?option=com_content&task=view&id=122&Itemid=50

112. http://contrib.andrew.cmu.edu/usr/es36/history/dates.html

113. Pittsburgh Post-Gazette, April 5, 1976, page 19

114. Pittsburgh Post Gazette, October 22, 1976, page 24

115. Pittsburgh Post-Gazette, October 22, 1976, page 23

116. http://www.post-gazette.com/pg/07227/809448-388.stm

1977

117. http://ech.case.edu/ech-cgi/article.pl?id=CN

117. New York Times (April 24, 1977) and Chronicle Telegraph (May 9, 1977)

118. Pittsburgh Post-Gazette, August 8, 1977 C-1

119. Pittsburgh Post-Gazette, September 9, 1977

1978

120. http://www41mania.com/wrestling/column/51581/Just-S/pose-3.18.07.htm

120. http://www.geocities.com/johnny_mongoose/pisces.html#didyouknow

121. Pittsburgh Post-Gazette, October 8, 1978

122. Pittsburgh Post-Gazette, December 29, 1978

1979

123. http://www.oursportscentral.com/misl/197879.html

124. http://www.piaa.org/champioships/archive/default.aspx

124. Pittsburgh Post-Gazette, March 25, 1979

125. Pittsburgh Post-Gazette, September 5, 1979

126. http://www.thewholive.de/konzerte/zeige_konzert.php?

126. www.crowdsafe.com/cafe/who20.html

126. www.narcosislabs.com/gOdsEzlcAntdAncE/Music/concerts.html

1980

127. http://www.contrib.andrew.cmu.edu/usr/es36/history/dates.html

127. Pittsburgh Post-Gazette, January 31, 1980

128. http://www.eastsideboxing.com/news.php?p=5544&more=1

128. http://www.hickoksports.com/boigraph/leonardsugarray.shtml

129. http://www.contrib.andrew.cmu.edu/usr/es36/history/dates.html

129. Pittsburgh Post-Gazette, December 15, 1980

Chapter 5, 1981-1985

1981

<u>129) March 7</u>

The Panthers prevail

The Pittsburgh Panthers men's basketball team defeated their cross town rivals the Duquesne Dukes 64-60 in the East Eight Tournament Final. The victory gave Pittsburgh an automatic NCAA bid.

The game wasn't exactly a classic as both teams combined for 50 turnovers (29 for Duquesne and 21 for Pitt). The crowd of 13,823 saw Pitt take an early 12-point lead then hung on the rest of the way. Ronnie Dixon had 20 points for the Dukes while Panther's Lennie McMillian matched those points and won the Tournament MVP. In the NCAA Tournament Pittsburgh made it to the second round but lost to eventual runner-ups North Carolina 74 to 57.

Did you know after his collegiate years with the Pittsburgh Panthers, Lennie McMillian played professional basketball in Ireland?

<u>130) March 13</u>

Revenge after 16 years

Were you there when the Uniontown Red Raiders (26-2) defeated Aliquippa Quips 80-67 to capture their fifth AAA WPIAL basketball championship? This would be sweet revenge for their stunning 1965 loss to the same team.

The Red Raiders were a small but quick team. They had the Quips on their heels virtually from the start of the game. Leading the way in front of a Civic Arena crowd of 9, 428 was Uniontown's Graig Harris with 22 points and 13 rebounds.

131) March 29

"The Great One" shines through

In hockey action the Edmonton Oilers humbled the Pittsburgh Penguins 5-2. On this night 20 year-old Wayne "The Great One" Gretzky collected three assists and in the process broke one NHL record and tied another. On his first assist he got point number 153 for the season (breaking Phil Esposito's mark of 152 in 77 games) and on the third assist he tied Bobby Orr's assist record of 102.

The 12, 966 gracious Pittsburgh fans acknowledged Gretzky on his points record with a 30-second standing ovation.

Did you know Wayne Gretzky's father Walter was in attendance this night? - 130

132) November 6

Controversy in the ring

In the battle of the undefeated boxers, Larry Holmes held off Renaldo Snipes in a controversial heavy weight boxing match. The fight for the WBC crown was the first world championships in Pittsburgh in 30 years.

From the beginning bell both boxers pounded each other with some forceful blows. In the 7th round Snipes actually put Holmes down but couldn't finish him off. Later in the 11th round Holmes stunned Snipes with a couple good whacks. The ref, feeling Snipes was hurt too bad stopped the match and awarded Holmes the victory by Technical Knock Out (TKO). Many of the 14,103 fans at the Civic Arena thought the call was pre-mature and booed the decision. Then seemingly out of nowhere chaos started in the ring. It seems Snipe's manager Nick Rattenni got into an argument with Jake Holmes (Larry's brother) and a melee ensued. Security guards and police were called into the fray as they tried to settle down the crowd. However amidst the pushing and shoving Rattenni's scissors cut a gash into Snipes left forearm that required 12 stitches. Finally, after several minutes of restraining, the police got control of the situation. For Snipes, it was a tough first loss, especially the part about being injured only after the fight.

In one of the under cards that night, 271 pound David "Hand Grenade" Bey defeated the young but undefeated James" Buster" Douglas in the second round via a TKO.

Did you know Larry Holmes was born in Cuthbert, Georgia but spent the most of his adult life in Easton, Pennsylvania? His nickname was the 'Easton Assassin.'

133) November 21

He's a one man wrecking crew!

In front of a record soccer crowd of 10,057 the Pittsburgh Spirit defeated the Philadelphia Fever 6 to 5. Pittsburgh forward and Polish National Star Stan Terlecki scored 4 goals and collects 2 assists for a 6 point night. Terlecki's 4 goals tied a team record while his 3 goals in the last period broke a team record.

Did you up to this point two other Spirit players had 4 goals in a game? They were Graham Fife and Steve Buttle.

134) November 23-24

"Even Now" I can pack the house

Were you there when Barry Manilow tickled the ivory in Steel Town? His 2 sold-out concerts were also aired nationally on the Showtime cable T.V. network. Barry sang many of his hits which included: I Write the Songs, Jump Shout Boogie, Can't Smile Without You, Weekend in New England and If I Should Love Again. He also did a medley with It's a Miracle, Daybreak, This One's for You, Looks Like We Made It, Could It Be Magic and Mandy. If you recall that evening, the stage was set up as a "theater in the round." The show-stopper came when Manilow performed Copacabana. During the song Barry wore a silver vest with puffy silver sleeves. Meanwhile he rode down the aisle in a cart with palm trees and drums painted on the side panels. When the song was over he took off his vest to reveal a Pittsburgh Steelers jersey with the number 12 on it (Terry Bradshaw). The crowd went absolutely berserk!

1982

135) March 6

The mountain men get mauled!

Led by Clyde Vaughan and Dwayne Wallace the Pittsburgh Panthers (19-9) defeated the West Virginia Mountaineers (26-2 and nationally ranked in the top ten) 79-72 to capture its second straight Eastern 8 Tournament title. This was also the final game ever played for the Eastern 8 Tournament. The attendance that night was 16,056.

Pittsburgh shot 67% in the second half while the Mountaineers ran into foul trouble all night. Dwayne Wallace finished the night with 20 points while teammate Clyde Vaughan had 21 points and 10 rebounds. For his tournament efforts Vaughan captured the MVP.

Did you know about 10 days before this contest West Virginia had beaten Pittsburgh at their home court in Morgantown? After that game Mountaineer Coach Gale Catlett called the Pittsburgh program "mediocre." I guess revenge is sweet.

136) April 2

A bittersweet win for Pennsylvania

On this night 14,326 people saw Team Pennsylvania defeat Team U.S. 91-85 in the Roundball Classic. This was significant because it was the last time Pennsylvania won the famed high school basketball game. Pennsylvania was led by Clairton's Lloyd Moore with 15 points while Chip Greenberg had 14 points, 3 assists and 3 steals and was named the MVP. The Pennsylvania coach Doug Masciola and player Rick Suder both represented Center High School.

Team U.S. was supposed to win especially with big Benoit Benjamin out of Monroe, Louisiana. He stood 7 feet tall and weighed 240 pounds. He was being recruited by every major college in the country but on this night he only managed 14 points.

Did you know there was a preliminary game this night? Ohio beat Pennsylvania 99 to 98 as they outscored the Keystoners 26 to 11 in the final quarter.

<u>137) April 9</u>

They were the best Police around!

At the height of their popularity the Police gave a clean, tight concert as part of the Ghost in the Machine Tour. Unfortunately the opening act that night was not so good. In fact a writer at the Pittsburgh Post-Gazette said it was the worse group ever with terrible singing and bad music playing. Their names: Bow Wow Wow!

Did you know Bow Wow Wow did have a hit with I Want Candy? It was originally recorded by the American group The Strangeloves in 1965 and made it to # 11 on the U.S. Hot 100 chart.

1983

<u>138) February 2-6</u>

They're skating circles around me!

On these dates the U.S. Figure Skating Championships were held at the Civic Arena for the first time in its history. The winners were the following: Ladies-gold medal = Rosalyn Summers, silver medal = Elaine Zayak, bronze medal = Tiffany Chin. For the 18 year-old Summers this was her second straight national title. Meanwhile Zayak who came in second was the defending World Champion. Chin gave a good showing for a 15 year-old and would later win the gold medal in 1985.

For the men-gold medal = Scott Hamilton, silver medal = Brian Boitano, bronze medal = Mark Cockerell. For Hamilton this was his third straight national title. Boitano would have to wait a couple more years before winning 4 straight U.S. championships. Cockerell would win another bronze medal the following year and a silver medal in the next one.

In the pairs it was gold medal = Caitlin "Kitty" Carruthers and Peter Carruthers, silver medal = Lee Ann Miller and William Fauver, bronze medal = Jill Watson and Burt Lancon. For Caitlin Carruthers and her adopted brother Peter this was their third consecutive gold medal as pairs at the U.S. championships. They would go on to win a fourth gold medal the following year. Miller and Fauver never won a U.S. pairs championship but in 4 years finished with 3 silvers and 1 bronze. For Watson and Lancon this was the first of 2 consecutive bronze medals. Later Watson would partner with Peter Oppegard and win 3 pairs gold medals and 1 silver.

In ice dancing the gold medal = Judy Blumberg and Michael Seibert, silver medal = Elisa Spitz and Scott Gregory, bronze medal = Carol Fox and Richard Dalley. For Blumberg and Seibert this was their third of five consecutive gold medals. Previously they had won a silver and bronze at the nationals. For Spitz and Gregory the silver medal was sandwiched between 2 bronze medals. Fox and Dalley would get their second bronze medal but also finished their careers with 5 silver medals in ice dancing.

Did you know Michael Seibert was born in Pittsburgh and he and his partner Judy Blumberg were members of the Pittsburgh Figure Skating Club?

139) December 27

Panthers are golden

Were you there when the Pittsburgh Panthers defeated Illinois State 59-54 in the championship game of the inaugural **Golden Triangle Classic** tournament? Despite the tight defensive battle, Panthers' George Allen and Clyde Vaughan collected 20 points each. Pittsburgh stymied Illinois several times in the last 6 minutes-not allowing them to score a single field goal!

Earlier in the tournament Pittsburgh beat cross town rivals Duquesne Dukes 64 to 59. Both Panther victories were come-from-behind ones.

1984

140) September 21-22

The Boss gets a birthday surprise

As part of his "Born In The U.S.A." tour Bruce Springsteen rocked the Civic Arena with 2 sold out concerts. The 17,000 plus fans got their money's worth as the three and a half hour marathon shows lasted past midnight. As usual Springsteen encouraged audience participation and at least one lucky fan got a thrill of a lifetime. While performing "Dancing in the Dark" the Boss had a young lady dance with him on stage.

On the night of the September 22nd show, Springsteen got a pleasant surprise. At midnight a birthday cake was passed from the audience to the stage. The band then started to play Happy Birthday to Bruce-his 35th.

Did you know the Boss turned 60 on September 23, 2009?

141) December 14

The youngsters get a kick out of it

On this night the Civic Arena hosted America's First National High School Indoor Soccer All-Star Match. The evening got started with a preliminary game that saw the Pittsburgh Area All-Stars take on the Cleveland Area All-Stars. Cleveland got off to a fast start and sustained pressure all game. When all was said and done they soundly beat Pittsburgh 8 to 3. Cleveland's Tommy O'Rourke, Angelo Catenacci and Michael Piro had 2 goals each. For his efforts Piro received honors as the offensive player of the game. Meanwhile, on the losing end, Moon's Steve Thomas had a pair for Pittsburgh.

The Cleveland side composed of players from the Northeast Ohio's prestigious East-West soccer club. They literally had been a team long before this All-Star match. Their superior chemistry definitely showed itself throughout the game.

In the second game, the pro-Pennsylvania crowd of 5,479 was hoping for some revenge as the U.S. All-Stars faced their Keystone state All-Stars. Team U.S. started strong and kept the Pennsylvania boys on their heels. As the match progressed the talent of the U.S. squad showed its true colors. By the end of the game they had walloped Pennsylvania 9 to 3. Herb Haler of Parma, Ohio scored 2 goals for Team U.S. and was named offensive star of the game. Moon's Sean Shapert-the nation's most prolific scholastic scorer with 213 goals had a pair for the losing side.

Did you know the Cleveland All-Stars beat the U.S. All-Stars 3 to 2 in a scrimmage game played 2 days before this event?

1985

142) January 12

Super Mario faces The Great One

Were you there when the Pittsburgh Penguins defeated the defending Stanley Cup Champs Edmonton Oilers 4-3? This was the first time superstars Mario Lemieux and Wayne Gretzky faced each other at the Civic Arena. The sold-out crowd was not disappointed as Lemieux ended the night with 2 goals while Gretzky had 3 assists.

<u>143) May 28</u>

Respect Yourself

As part of her "Virgin Tour" Madonna played to a sold out Civic Arena crowd. Many of the teenage girls and even a couple guys dressed from head to toe like their music hero. As for the "Material Girl" herself, she was decked out in a multi-colored jacket on top and a mini-skirt over a biker style racing shorts on the bottom. Her accessories included fingerless gloves, high-top black shoes and loads of make-up. One Post-Gazette writer called her attire "Trash with flash." While singing "Like a Virgin" Madonna sported a short white wedding dress, white shoes and a bouquet.

Along with her varied costumes Madonna also had quite a unique stage setup. It featured more than 100 overhead lights on trusses, flown speakers, black light, dry ice smoke and white balloons. The balloons were inscribed with the words "Dreams Come True" and were released during the song "Angel".

For Madonna fans, this was the first and only time the "Material Girl" played at the Civic Arena. If you were there early you may recall the opening act. It was the Beastie Boys.

Did you know Madonna's father Silvio, grew up in West Aliquippa?

1981

129. http://pittsburghpanthers.cstv.com/trads/pitt-trads-timelines.html

130. Pittsburgh Post-Gazette, March 15, 1981

131. Peter Gzowski, *The Game of Our Lives*, Toronto, Ontario, Canada, McClelland and Stewart Limited 1981.

132. http://www.ringsidereport.com/Henderson5112006.htm

133. Pittsburgh Post-Gazette, November 22, 1981

134. http://www.hiponline.com/artist/music/m/manilow/barry/

134. http://www.barrynet.com/bn321981.html

1982

135. http://pittsburghpanthers-cstv.com/trads/pitt-trads-timelines.html

135. Pittsburgh Post-Gazette, March 7, 1982

136. www.RoundballClassic.net

137. Pittsburgh Post Gazette, April 10, 1982

1983

138. New York Times, February 4, 1983, Section A, Page 22

138. The Washington Post, February 6, 1983, H14

139. Pittsburgh Post-Gazette, December 28, 1983

1984

140. What are your memories of Mellon Arena? Pittsburgh Post-Gazette, January 21, 2007

140. en.wikipedia.org/wiki/Bruce_Springsteen

141. Pittsburgh Post Gazette, December 15, 1984

1985

142. http://mysite.verizon.net/vze7m9n/id20.html

143. en.wikipedia.org/wiki/List_of_Madonna_concert_tours

143. What are your memories of Mellon Arena? Pittsburgh Post-Gazette, January 21, 2007

Chapter 6, 1986-1990

1986

<u>144) April 6</u>

A Classic gets a make-over

On this night the Dapper Dan Roundball Classic changed its format for the first time in 22 years. Since its inception in 1965, the Classic had a preliminary local All-Star game followed by Team Pennsylvania taking on Team U.S. This time to shake things up a bit, organizers added an extra game. After the preliminary one, fans saw Team U.S. South challenge Team U.S. North and in the finale Team U.S. East battled Team Pennsylvania.

When the first game started fans saw a real nail-biter as Western Pennsylvania Interscholastic Athletic League (WPIAL) beat City-West Penn 78-77. In the next one, the game again went down to the wire as Team U.S. South edged Team U.S. North 96-94. As fans caught their breath the third game was on deck. This time Pennsylvania pride was on the line. Would they beat the best from the U.S. East? As the teams took to the hard court anticipation at the Civic Arena was building. The game got underway and both teams brought their A game. Buckets were being drained on both sides. The score, like the first two games could be determined by a bucket or less. The teams continued to exchange points until the end. When the final buzzer sounded Team U.S. East eked out a victory 98 to 96.

Though all three games were exciting to watch, the attendance faltered. The crowd of just over 8,000 was the lowest ever in the event history. Some blamed it on the fact that Team Pennsylvania did not have a marquee player while others pointed to time of the games-Sunday afternoon. Whatever the reason, organizers would again change the format the following year. This time, like the first 21 years of the Roundball Classic, only one game would be played after the preliminary one. It would feature Team East versus Team West. Team Pennsylvania would not be part of the billing and as a result future attendance waned.

145) April 12

The final "KISS?"

The 6,192 fans that came out this night saw the final performance of the KISS "Asylum Tour". The tour, which started on November 29, 1985, included 91 shows. One special moment came at the closing of the spectacle. As part of the end-tour pranks the road crew came on stage and did a chorus line during "Lick It Up".

Did you know this concert was originally scheduled for April 3 but something happened to the venue? On that night thousands of fans showed up but were turned away when an electrical transformer blew out at the Civic Arena.

146) October 6

This monkey business is pretty profitable!

The place looked like a barrel of Monkees. Twenty years after their first concert at the Civic Arena the Monkees returned on their "20th Anniversary North American Tour". The Monkees proved so popular that every concert on this tour was sold out. In fact it was the largest grossing tour of 1986.

On this night Mickey Dolenz, Davy Jones and Peter Tork were jumping and dancing up a storm. Their infectious energy kept the audience engaged continuously. The band also threw in their share of corny jokes which lightened the mood. As for the music, it was tight. Even critics would have been impressed.

Mike Nesmith was not part of the group for this concert. He did however join the boys for a few gigs on the tour.

Did you know the other bands on stage that night were: Herman's Hermits, the Grass Roots and Gary Puckett and the Union Gap?

1987

147) January 30

The AHL returns with a familiar brother

The Baltimore Skipjacks (Pittsburgh Penguins farm team) defeated the Sherbrooke Canadiens (Montreal Canadiens farm team) 4 to 3. The game marked the first time in 20 years since an American Hockey League game was played at the Civic Arena. Alain Lemieux, Mario's older brother, was named first star of the game as he scored 2 goals for the Skipjacks. The 5, 383 fans were appreciative especially Mario who was in attendance.

Did you know former Penguin player Gene Ubriaco was coach of the Baltimore Skipjacks?

148) June 19

Football makes its debut…on a 50 yard field!

Were you among the 12,117 when the Pittsburgh Gladiators defeated the Washington Commandos 48-46 in the first ever regular season game of the new Arena Football League (AFL)? Mike Hohensee (Gladiator quarterback) threw the first touchdown in league history when he completed a 42-yarder to Russell Hairston.

Though the beginning of this game was exciting, the ending was even wilder. The Gladiators actually scored the winning touchdown on a broken play. Leading 42 to 40 at the time, Pittsburgh tried a 36 yard field goal with 2:14 remaining. The kick by Lee Larson was wide but the ball hit the end nets. As it dropped to the ground it was considered a loose ball. Another Gladiator jumped on it in the end zone and the referee signaled a touchdown. However with a minute left in the game the Commandos responded with their own touchdown. Being down only 2 points, Washington kicker Dale Castro then attempted a dropkick extra-point worth 2 points. He missed and the Gladiators claimed victory in their home opener.

Did you know Mike Hohensee was also the first player to be drafted in the first AFL draft?

149) August 1

Dynamite blows Gladiators away

On this day the Denver Dynamite destroyed the Pittsburgh Gladiators 45-16 in Arena Bowl 1. Unfortunately for Pittsburgh fans the game was a laugher. Denver was so dominant the score was 32 to 0 by the end of the 3rd quarter. Defensively, the Dynamite proved just as strong with 10 sacks. The MVP went to Denver's Gary Mullen who caught 9 passes including 3 for touchdowns.

Though the 13, 232 home town fans were disappointed, they did at least become part of something significant. They witnessed the only game in AFL history to be played in an open air environment-yes the Civic Arena dome was retracted for this special contest!

Did you know the Pittsburgh Gladiators played three more years in the AFL before moving south to become the Tampa Bay Storm in 1991?

1988

150) February 10

Orangemen leave Panthers feeling blue

The No.12 ranked Syracuse Orangemen (18-5) defeated the Pittsburgh Panthers (18-7) 84-75 in one of the biggest hyped basketball games of the season. It was supposed to be a battle of the big 3 of Syracuse-Rony Seiklay, Derrick Coleman and Sherman Douglas versus the big 3 of Pittsburgh-Charles Smith, Jerome Lane and Sean Miller. Ironically it was little known Matt Roe of Syracuse who stole the show. He scored 11 points early in the first quarter and added 14 more to lead all shooters that night with 25. He definitely was the difference maker.

Unfortunately for Pittsburgh this was a bad night on two accounts. First, they lost the game and secondly, they did it in front of 16,798 spectators-the largest crowd ever to witness a basketball contest in Pittsburgh history. There was however, one consolation for the Panthers that evening. Jerome Lane became the 16th player in Pittsburgh history to score 1,000 points or more.

Did you know the day after this game (Feb. 11) the Duquesne Dukes (Pittsburgh's other basketball team) drew only 843 fans to the Civic Arena? At least they beat Rutgers 73 to 58.

151) February 20

Things get nasty on the hardwood

On this night of basketball the game actually ended before regulation time expired. The scene, in front of 16,721-the second largest to date for a basketball game in Pittsburgh had the Panthers leading Georgetown Hoyas 70-65 with 4 seconds to play. The Panthers were ready to take some foul shots when one of the Georgetown players threw an intentional elbow to the back of Pittsburgh's Jerome Lane. A fight started and a bench clearing brawl ensued. Soon players, fans and the police all got involved. Eventually Georgetown coach John Thompson took his players to the locker room and never returned.

After this incident and others like it in 1988, the NCAA instituted new rules regarding fighting in basketball.

Did you know in a game played between Pittsburgh and Georgetown on January 6 of the same year (at the Capital Center in Washington), Mark Tillmon of the Hoyas was ejected for elbowing a Panther player? Obviously there is no love lost between these teams!

152) September 26-28

The "King of Pop' packs 'em in

After performing in Europe for almost 4 months Michael Jackson made Pittsburgh his first stop on his return to his "Bad" tour in the U.S. Ironically this was the first and only time the "King of Pop" performed at the Civic Arena as a solo artist. The attendance for the three sold out shows was an astounding 48,690!

Jackson didn't disappoint his loyal fans as he sang and danced like no other. He performed his famous moonwalk and even grabbed his crotch while performing the song "Human Nature"-go figure. If you were at any of these concerts you may recall that Jackson made several costume changes throughout the show.

Some fanatics of Jackson tried to see him at his hotel in Pittsburgh. Fortunately for Michael his entourage guarded his whereabouts brilliantly. As one Pittsburgh Post-Gazette reporter stated "Jackson's security was tighter than his pants"

Did you know one of Jackson's backup singers was Sheryl Crow?

153) December 16

A Rocky Mountain High hits Pittsburgh

John Denver delighted 9,327 concert goers and a few more. This was a televised Christmas Special that also featured special guest singers. One of the performers was nine year old local singer Melodee Lynn. She was among 39 grade-school children from Elm Grove Elementary School in McMurray, Pa. They helped Denver in singing 6 Christmas songs including Rudolph the Red-Nosed Reindeer and Away in a Manger. The show was actually divided in two with John playing his hits in the first part and then switching to Christmas ones in the second half.

The last song performed that evening was Falling Leaves (The Refugees) which no one had heard before. Denver had audience members hold hands as he taught them the lyrics.

Did you know Denver's musicians James Burton, Jerry Scheff and Glen D. Hardin all played for Elvis in his heyday?

154) December 31

Super Mario puts on a good "end of the year" show

On this New Year's Eve at the Civic Arena the Pittsburgh Penguins took on division rivals the New Jersey Devils. Mario Lemieux put on an offensive show that got him into the record books. He scored 5 goals in 5 different ways-power play, even strength, short-handed, penalty shot and empty net. He was and still is the only player in NHL history to accomplish this feat. In the same game Lemieux also collected 3 assists for an 8-point night-not too shabby for a year-end performance! By the way Pittsburgh won the game 8-6.

1989

155) January 4

Penguins do it "Army style"

Pittsburgh hockey fans got a taste of international play this night. The Pittsburgh Penguins faced the mighty Moscow Central Red Army team in front of 12,309 curious onlookers. Mario Lemieux stood tall again as he scored once and collected two assists. Meanwhile present day color commentator Bob

Errey (Root Sports) had one goal and one assist as the Penguins handed the Red Army a 4-2 loss.

In 1989 the Red Army hockey team played 7 exhibition games against various NHL squads. They finished with a record of 4 wins, 1 tie and 2 losses.

Did you know the Moscow Central Red Army hockey club had won 12 straight national championships up to this point?

156) April 2-3

"Deadheads" do some damage.

These 2 sold-out Grateful Dead concerts proved to be some of the wildest scenes at a Civic Arena event ever. It started when 12,000 to 15,000 Deadheads camped out in cars, vans and tents in the surrounding area. Some even paid the Civic Arena Corp. $24.00 to camp in parking lots from April 2 (Sunday morning) to midnight on April 3. In the two days police towed away almost 100 vehicles parked illegally near the arena.

Before the second day show about 500 Deadheads tried to crash the concert without tickets. At one point they started throwing rocks and beer bottles (empty and full ones) as a police officer was handcuffing a guy for trying to crash a gate. As the melee persisted further action had to be taken. Soon 60 police officers were called to the Civic Arena parking lot to restore order. After sorting through the chaos, a total of 31 people were arrested. The breakdown included: 16 for public intoxication, 8 on drug charges and 7 for various offenses such as assault, disorderly conduct, criminal mischief, resisting arrest and indecent exposure. What a night at the Igloo!

Did you know Pittsburgh Mayor Sophie Masloff upon reviewing the incidents on TV was quoted as saying "I don't want those Deadenders ever back again?" The group is fine, but those people who follow them around are not."

157) April 7

A "Shaq" attack is not enough!

In the 25th annual Dapper Dan Roundball Classic the East took on the best from the West. Led by Billy McCaffrey from Allentown Central Catholic, the East jumped out to a 20-0 lead and never looked back. McCaffrey finished the game with 14 points, 4 assists and 3 steals and was named his teams' MVP as the East held off the West 96-84. The 12, 378 fans in attendance got a glimpse of some future college and NBA stars in the likes of Bobby Hurley, Jimmy Jackson and slam dunk wizard Harold Miner. However the class of the field was a 7-footer from San Antonio called Shaquille O'Neal. O'Neal was the best player on the West with 18 points and 14 rebounds. Though his team lost, he grabbed the West MVP honors.

Did you know Shaquille O'Neal played his first pro contest in Pittsburgh on October 20, 2009? His Cleveland Cavaliers destroyed the Dallas Mavericks in a pre-season game 96-66 at the Peterson Event Center on the campus of the University of Pittsburgh.

158) April 25

Another day at the office for Mario

In a high scoring NHL playoff game the Pittsburgh Penguins outlasted the Philadelphia Flyers 10-7. Mario Lemieux tied 4 NHL play-off records when he: scored 5 goals in one game, scored 4 in one period, collected 8 points in one game and obtained 4 points in one period.

If you were at the game you may recall what happened when Pittsburgh's Rob Brown made the score 9-2. Flyers goalie Ron Hextall was so angry he chased Brown around the ice.

The Pens victory gave them a 3-2 series lead and confidence to eliminate Philly in the next game. However, the pesky Flyers roared back to win the next 2 games beating out Pittsburgh in 7 games.

Did you know in the 1988-89 NHL regular season Mario Lemieux won the scoring race with 199 points?

159) November 24

Panthers leave Soviet Army red-faced

In an international exhibition basketball game the Pittsburgh Panthers took care of the bigger but much slower Soviet Red Army team 108-89. Pittsburgh used their speed early and often as they converted on a number of fast breaks. Darelle Porter led the way with 8 assists on the Panthers first 9 baskets. The Soviets who boasted 7-foot 2, 303-pound giant Vladimar Tkachenko ran into foul trouble all night in trying to tame the slick running Panthers. In fact four Soviets fouled out as referees called a total of 70 fouls in the rough game. The Panthers got good production from Rod Brookin, Brian Shorter and Jason

Matthews as they netted 27, 26 and 24 points respectively. The Red Army team was led by Sergey Tarakanov with 18.

Did you know the Russian assistant coach Ivan Edeshko had the winning assist in the Soviets upset victory over the U.S. in the 1972 Summer Olympics in Munich?

160) December 26

Some famous boys hit the mats

Were you there to see the "World Grand Championships" of Wrestling? If so, you were among 9,690 spectators-the largest to witness an Olympic style wrestling event in the U.S. On this night 11 matches were fought between Team U.S. Wrestlers and the World Wrestlers (including 8 from the Soviet Union). A total of $65,000 was awarded in prize money to the participants. In one of the highlights for Team U.S., Kenny Monday (Olympic and World champion) defeated Soviet Union star Nasyr Gadzhikanov (1989 European Champion) 7-0. Monday received $4,000 for winning his match and an additional $5,000 for being named the Outstanding Wrestler in the competition. In a much closer match 286-pound American Bruce Baumgartner (and former gold medalist) defeated David Gobedjishvili of the Soviet Union 4 to 3. Ironically Baumgartner lost to Gobedjishvili in the gold medal match at the 1988 Seoul Olympics. In the main event 24-year old American John Smith and Olympic and 2-time World champion defeated Sergei Beloglazov who was not only a 2-time Olympic winner but was also a 6-time World champion. The 33-year old Beloglazov was probably not in top form as he just came out of retirement. Smith won the match 6 to 2.

1990

161) January 3

A seesaw battle 'til the end

On this day the Syracuse Orangemen (the Associated Press poll No.1 team) took on the Pittsburgh Panthers in a classic men's basketball game at the Igloo. Early in the game Pittsburgh looked comfortable with an 18 to 5 lead. However, the Orangemen rallied several times including being down 3 points (67 to 64) then later 5 points (72-67). Syracuse also had 30 offensive rebounds to Pitt's 7 but their best play may have been a defensive one. With the game winding down and being down by one (78-77) LeRon Ellis (6'10") blocked a layup by Panther Jason Matthews. Ellis then picked up the rebound, threw it up court to Stephen Thompson (24 points) who converted a 3 point play with 5 seconds left in the game. With the score 80-78 for Syracuse the stunned crowd of 16,188 still thought there was a chance to win though time was against them. After getting the ball quickly back up court Pitt's Brian Shorter's took a 19-foot shot. The ball was headed toward the net with 1 second left in the game. It hit the front rim and bounced away. The game was over and shock filled the air.

162) January 5

Blazers "Bull"ied around

The Pittsburgh Bulls defeated the New England Blazers 14-11 on a night fans were introduced to a new sport. This was the first professional lacrosse game ever played at the Civic Arena. The crowd of 9,213 saw Brian Nikula score Pittsburgh's first ever goal just 60 seconds into the contest. He later tallied 3 more and added 2 assists for a 6-point night. For his efforts Nikula was named the game's MVP.

The Bulls would go on to play 4 years in the Major Indoor Lacrosse League before folding at the end of the 1993 season.

Did you know in1990 Brian Nikula (New Westminster, B.C.) of the Bulls led the league in goals with 20?

163) January 21

Mario was the brightest star

In the 41st NHL All-Star Game and the first one ever held at the Civic Arena the Wales Conference humbled the Campbell's Conference 12-7. Mario Lemieux scored 4 goals and was named the games' MVP. The game saw the following records broken. Most goals scored in an All-Star game by both teams (19). Most goals scored in a game by one team (12) and most goals scored in one period by one team (7). Also for the first time in All-Star history there was an All-Star Weekend. Included was a Heroes of Hockey (old-timers) game plus an NHL All-Star Skills Competition. Furthermore, during the actual All-Star game, referees, head coaches and other on ice officials were miked. Finally NBC who broadcasted the game in the U.S. did player interviews during stoppages during the game. The attendance of 17, 503 included Buffalo Bills quarterback Jim Kelly.

Did you know Mario Lemieux's 4 goals tied him with Wayne Gretzky (1983) for the most goals in an All-Star game? Lemieux's 3 goals in the first period, however was an All-Star record.

164) February 4-5

An ex Beatle gets back to the 'Burgh

Were you there when Paul McCartney played 2 sold-out concerts from his "Get Back World Tour"? This was the first time since September 14, 1964 that a member from the Beatles performed at the Civic Arena.

McCartney's repertoire this night included 14 songs from the Beatles like Yesterday, Back in the USSR, Sgt. Pepper's Lonely Hearts Club Band, The Long and Winding Road, Let It Be and Get Back. He also played 10 songs from his various solo albums like: Ebony and Ivory, Live and Let Die and Coming Up. One of the crowd's favorite moments of the evening came with Hey Jude which turned into a sing-a-long.

Did you know Paul McCartney's former wife Linda played keyboards with the band?

165) June 29

Birthday boy gets a kick

In a high scoring arena football game, the Denver Dynamite squeaked by the Pittsburgh Gladiators 47-45 in dramatic style. Dynamite kicker Tracy Bennet booted a 52-yard field goal with 2 seconds left in the game as the stunned crowd of 4,869 looked on. Bennet had a double reason to celebrate-the victory and it was his 22nd birthday!

If you were at this game you may recall the roof being opened briefly in the third quarter.

Did you know Dynamite kicker Tracy Bennet made 7 field goal attempts this game? Only the last one was good.

166) September 22

That's a lot of Bull!

On this fall day, the Miller High Life Championship Rodeo kicked into town. The show featured various events such as bareback and saddle bronc riding, calf roping, steer wrestling and bull riding. The event was marred when a 1,900 pound bull named the "Bucking Machine" broke its leg on the first ride and had to be eventually put down. After the rodeo left town, Pittsburgh city council introduced laws that limited restrictive devices on show animals. When these new regulations came into effect the Civic/Mellon Arena never hosted another rodeo show ever.

Did you know before this event, 40 animal right activists protested outside the Civic Arena?

167) December 15

Michael got more mojo!

Michael Moorer from Monessen, PA defended his World Boxing Organization (WBO) light heavyweight title against Canadian Danny Stonewalker in an eighth round stoppage. The decisive hit occurred when Moorer drove a hard right hand punch to Stonewalker's mid section that put him down. The ref called the bout since Stonewalker had been floored 4 times including 3 in the last 2 rounds. Earlier in the 5th round Moorer's right hand blow split Stonewalker's nose. Moorer's victory would keep his record perfect (22-0) while Stonewalker dropped to 15-6-1.

In a short but furious preliminary bout Gerald McClellan disposed of Pittsburgh native Dan Mitchell in the first round.

Did you know Danny Stonewalker was a Cree Indian?

1986

144. Pittsburgh Post-Gazette, April 7, 1986

145. Curt Gooch, Jeff Suhs, *Kiss Alive Forever: The Complete Touring History,* New York, Billboard Books, 2002.

146. www.monkeeland.com/Timeline/66.html

146. en.wikipedia.org/wiki/The_Monkees

1987

147. http://www.contrib.andrew.cmu.edu/usr/es36/history/dates.html

148. www.arenafan.com/teams/?page=history&team=5&year=1987

148. Pittsburgh Post-Gazette, June 20, 1987, page 1&3

149. http://www.40brinkster.com/drsmitty/AFL/AFL.html

1988

150. http://pqasb.pqarchiver.com/latimes/access/58831382.html?dids=58831382:58831382&
FMTS=ABS:FT&date=Feb

150. Pittsburgh Post-Gazette, February 11, 1988

151. New York Times, January 7 & February 22, 1988

151. Miami Herald, February 26, 1988

152. www.halfvalue.com/wiki.jsp?topic=Bad_World_Tour

152. Pittsburgh Post-Gazette, September 29, 1988 D-1

153. Valley Independent, December 12, 1988

153. profile.myspace.com/index.cfm?fuseaction=user.viewprofile&friend=27587580

153. www.shellworld.net/~emily/nws/jan1997.nws

154. http://www.contrib.andrew.cmu.edu/usr/es36/history/dates.html

1989

155. http://mysite.verizon.net/vze7mp9n/id20.html

156. http://www.bmusic.com.au/links/whatsnew/newsletters/archives/newsno9.html

157. http://www.pahoops.org/gyms.htm

158. http://en.wikipedia.org/wiki/1988-89_Pittsburgh_penguins_season

158. http://www.geocities.com/anduril66/lemieux.htm

159. Pittsburgh Post-Gazette, November 24&25

160. http://www.wrestlinginformation.com.
news-monday_vs_gadzhikanov_is_the_new_bout_of_the_week_on_usa_.html

1990

161. http://www.orangehoops.org/GameResults/G1989-1990.htm

162. www.geocities.com/Colosseum/Arena/6929/mill.html

163. http://music.musictnt.com/biography/41st_National_Hockey_League_All-Star_Game

163. http://en.wikipedia.org/wiki/41st_National_Hockey_League_All-Star Game

164. en.wikipedia.org/wiki/Get_Back_World_Tour

165. www.arenafan.com/teams/?page=history&team=5&year=1990

165. Pittsburgh Post Gazette, June 30, 1990

166. Pittsburgh Post-Gazette, September 20&24, 1990

166. The Valley Independent, September 24, 1990

167. http://nl.newsbank.com/nl-search/we/Archives?p_action=list&p_topdog=101+111

Chapter 7, 1991-1995

1991

<u>168) May 15</u>

Penguins "Final"ly see stars in their eyes

Were you there when the Minnesota North Stars stunned the Pittsburgh Penguins 5-4? This was the first ever Stanley Cup Final game played at the Civic Arena. The Penguins squandered many chances this game especially on the power-play. They managed only 1 goal on 8 tries. Even Pens young star Mark Recchi had his 14-game scoring streak stopped this night. The North Stars, meanwhile, played a tight defensive game and smothered the Pens on numerous occasions. Their leader Bobby Smith scored the winning goal.

Despite the loss, the Penguins led by coach Bob Johnson won the next 4 out of 5 games and captured the Stanley Cup for the first time in franchise history. In the final game of the series the Penguins walloped the North Stars 8-0 in Minnesota.

Did you Bob Johnson died later that year of brain cancer? Ironically, Bob Gainey, the North Star coach at the time and former player and later manager of the Montreal Canadiens lost his wife Cathy on June 21, 1995 after a 5-year battle with brain cancer. Gainey's 25 year-old daughter Laura died also when she was swept overboard during a sailing expedition in the North Atlantic on December 8, 2006. Her body was never recovered.

169) August 11

Two cups of ice in one day

The Hall of Fame/Canada Cup exhibit came to the 'Burgh. Hockey fans got a double treat this day as they were able to take pictures of the recently won Stanley Cup in the Igloo room while on the ice surface folks got to see two practice sessions by Team USA for the upcoming 1991 Canada Cup Hockey Tournament. Players were put through their paces by legendary coach Bob Johnson who at the time was also the Pittsburgh Penguin bench boss. Johnson's workouts were quite unique as he wore a microphone and explained to the spectators what his strategy would be.

Did you know Team USA practiced a full week at the Civic Arena before playing Team Canada in an exhibition game on August 19th? Team Canada won the game 6 to 2.

170) August 31

"Swede" victory!

Team USA defeated Team Sweden 6-3 in their first game of the Canada Cup Hockey Tournament. This was the only game played at the Civic Arena as part of this international competition. Instead of being upbeat about the start of this special event the American hockey team and the 13,676 fans in attendance were rather subdued. The reason, Bob Johnson head coach of the U.S. squad who just happened to be coach of the 1991 Stanley Cup champions Pittsburgh Penguins was in hospital with a brain tumor. As a result heavy hearts, tears and fears were part of the atmosphere. Before the puck was dropped public announcer John Barbero read a message wishing Bob Johnson well. In addition, concerned fans signed a big get-well card in the Civic Arena lobby for their ill coach.

After a predictable slow start to the game, Team USA got on track with 3 unanswered goals. Feisty Jeremy Roenick led the way with a pair while current Pens assistant coach Tony Granato netted one. With momentum on their side the Americans continued their onslaught as Brett Hull and Chris Chelios scored singles. By the end of the second period Team USA had a commanding 5-0 lead. The Swedes got 3 back in the third period but Graig Janney sealed the deal with the sixth American goal.

As a consolation prize for Team Sweden, Ulf Samuelsson was named his team's player of the game. Local hockey fans knew him well as he was a member of the Pittsburgh Penguins.

Did you know Team Canada won the Canada Cup by defeating Team USA 2 games to 0 in the best of three final series?

171) November 27

An American hockey legend is honored

The Pittsburgh Penguins doubled up the New Jersey Devils 8-4 before a capacity crowd of 16,164.Though the victory was sweet fans were pre-occupied with heavy thoughts this night. Before the game the Penguins honored deceased coach Bob Johnson, the only Penguin coach to that point to have won a Stanley Cup for Pittsburgh, in a 10 minute battery-operated candlelight ceremony. Johnson died the day before (November 26) at his home in Colorado Springs of brain cancer. He was 60 years old and was survived by his wife Martha and son Mark (former gold medalist in the 1980 Winter Olympics). As part of the ceremony a soloist sang The Lord's Prayer while the conclusion came with the playing of Linda Ronstadt's' "Goodbye My Friend".

"Badger Bob" entered the United States Hockey Hall of Fame in 1991 and in 1992 entered both the Hockey Hall of Fame and the Pittsburgh Penguins one. Fans and coaches will always remember him for his optimism and his famous saying "It's a great day for hockey!"-which by the way was painted beneath the ice surface just behind both blue lines on the night of his ceremony and kept there for the remaining of the season.

Did you know for the 2008-09 season, the Pittsburgh Penguins used the saying "A Great Day For Hockey" as their marketing slogan?

1992

172) April 3

Some Pittsburgh athletes are "Glad" to compete

The "American Gladiators Live" hit the Igloo with force this night. The 2-hour contest, based on a version of the "American Gladiators" as seen on T.V. after "Saturday Night Live", tested the abilities of some locals. Twelve of Pittsburgh's best athletes competed in feats of strength and agility against the traveling gladiator entourage that included: Chuck "Viper" Berlinger, Laser, Nitro, Turbo and Storm.

In order to have competed against the Gladiators hopefuls first had to participate in tryouts at the Civic Arena held on March 22, 1992. Three of the local Pittsburgh athletes were Jason Wick (Green Tree), Chelle Simons (Geneva College) and Beth Amato (Plum). Amato won her portion of the competition and was later featured on an "American Gladiators" show that was aired in September 1994.

173) April 23

Scotty, take a "Bow, man!"

The Pittsburgh Penguins defeated the Washington Capitals 6-4 in first round play-off action. After being down 2 games to 0 the Penguins scratched and clawed their way back into the series. The 16,164 fans saw a great solo performance while witnessing a brilliant coach break an NHL record. On the ice Mario Lemieux displayed his usual genius once again by figuring in all his team's goals. His 3 goals (including an empty-netter) and 3 assists highlighted a rough and tough contest that featured 20 penalties in the third period alone. Meanwhile behind the bench Penguin head coach Scotty Bowman became the most victorious coach in NHL playoff history. He got his 115th win thus surpassing Al Arbour who had 114-all with the New York Islanders.

Did you know the Pittsburgh Penguins would go on to defeat the pesky Washington Capitals 4 games to 3 and make it all the way to the Stanley Cup Finals?

174) May 26

Penguins make record comeback

Were you there when the Pittsburgh Penguins played one of their best playoff games ever? It was Game 1 of the 1992 Stanley Cup Finals and the Pens faced the surprising Chicago Blackhawks. Chicago rode an 11-game winning streak (an NHL playoff record at the time) and was hungry to win their first league title since 1961. Coached by the tough Mike Keenan and led by star Jeremy Roenick the Hawks were anxious to make a good first impression.

From the get go the boys from the windy city jumped all over the Pens and built a comfortable 4-1 lead. The home town fans stunned, wondered if their team could mount a comeback. As the game progressed however, the Penguins chipped away at the lead. They eventually scored 3 unanswered goals to tie the contest and dreamed of an overtime win. As regulation time winded down both teams wanted to win but didn't want to make any defensive mistakes.

With less than a minute to go defenseman Larry Murphy took a blast hoping for a miracle. Belfour stopped the shot but left a juicy rebound. Mario Lemieux jumped on the biscuit and fired it home. The crowd erupted as the roof almost came off the joint. The Pens held on to win the hard fought battle 5-4 and became the first team ever to overcome a 4-1 deficit in a Stanley Cup Final.

Filled with confidence the Penguins won the next three games as they swept the Blackhawks 4-0 to win their second Stanley Cup in a row.

Did you know the next time the Pittsburgh Penguins and the Chicago Blackhawks met in a Stanley Cup Finals was in the 1995 movie 'Sudden Death' starring Jean Claude Van Damme?

175) August 22

A cup full of summer fun

The "Penguins Summer Carnival" put a lot of smiles on faces this day. For the second year in a row the Penguin faithful got to rejoice in hockey supremacy. Fans joined players from the 2-time Stanley Cup winning team at the Civic Arena to celebrate and get some mementos. Penguins such as: Ron Francis, Troy Loney, Phil Bourque, Shawn McEachern, Jim Paek and Paul Stanton showed their appreciation by signing autographs for the appreciative crowd. In addition fans were able to take photographs of: the Stanley Cup and life-size cutouts of Jaromir Jagr and Mario Lemieux. There were also tours of the Penguins' locker room while prizes were given out at the game booth.

176) October 17

This "Coffey" is the best!

Were you there when the Pittsburgh Penguins defeated the New York Islanders 8-5? Paul Coffey of the Penguins broke two NHL defenseman records in one game. His first point of the game gave him career assist number 743-one better than legendary Islander great Dennis Potvin. His second assist gave him career point 1,053 also one better than Dennis Potvin. Ironically Coffey would still be one goal shy of Dennis Potvin's career goal amount of 310. However, the smooth skating defenseman later broke that record also. Upon retirement in 2001 Coffey had amassed 1,531 career points-second best for any NHL defenseman.

Did you know former Boston Bruin/Colorado Avalanche star Raymond Bourque leads all defensemen in career points with 1,579?

1993

177) April 10

The "March of the Penguins"

The Pittsburgh Penguins disposed of the New York Rangers 4-2 in front of a sold-out crowd of 16,164. This was not just another victory but the Penguins 17th consecutive one which established a new NHL record. The winning streak which started on March 9, 1993 lasted 32 days. During the record run, the Penguins outscored their opponents 98 to 48. The 17 victories included 10 wins at home and 7 on the road. The Penguins next and final game of the season on April 14, 1993 ended in a 6-6 overtime draw with the New Jersey Devils (no shoot outs at the time).

Did you know Mario Lemieux's 16-game scoring streak ended the night the Penguins won their 17th game in a row? Lemieux amassed an amazing 51 points during this run.

178) May 1

This graduation ceremony had a "Neighborhood" feeling to it!

Were you there for this special University of Pittsburgh's Graduation Ceremony? The guest speaker was one of Pittsburgh's (Latrobe) famous sons Mr. Fred Rogers. As Mr. Rogers entered the stage and walked toward the podium the school band played the theme song from "Mr. Rogers Neighborhood". Upon hearing the music, Mr. Rogers responded "Would you like to sing with me?" Then word for word the 2,000 graduates joined him and sang "Won't You Be My Neighbor?" Afterwards, Mr. Rogers received a rousing standing ovation.

When Mr. Rogers addressed the audience he gave a moving speech about the choices we make in life. Specifically he talked about a young man who overcame many challenges in his life to later become an outstanding citizen.

During this graduation ceremony Mr. Rogers received an honorary degree in public service.

Did you know Fred Rogers died on February 27, 2003 at the age of 74? His award winning children's show "Mr. Roger's Neighborhood" aired on 300 public TV stations from 1967 to 2000. The city of Pittsburgh honored Mr. Rogers with a statue in 2009.

179) May 14

One shot kills "three-peat"!

Were you there when the N.Y. Islanders upset the Pittsburgh Penguins in Game 7 of the Patrick Division Finals? This was one of the most disheartening losses in franchise history. The Penguins had the best regular season record in 1993 (119 points) and were also the two-time defending Stanley Cup Champs. After winning the first round playoff series against the New Jersey Devils (and their ninth consecutive one in 3 years) they faced the Islanders in the Patrick Division Finals. Leading the series 3-2 the Pens lost game 6 at Nassau Coliseum in New York. Confidence was still high though as Mario and teammates returned to the Civic Arena for game 7.

The contest was a nail biter as fans witnessed two teams facing elimination. The Islanders played a tight checking game keeping the Pens off balanced for most of the game. Trailing 3-1 late in the third period Pittsburgh desperately tried to get back into it. Ron Francis scored to close the gap and then with 60 seconds left Rick Tocchet deflected another one in that sent the crowd into a wild frenzy. With the scored tied 3-3 Penguin fans had confidence on their side. The game ended and overtime was coming up. The Penguins continued pressing early in the extra frame but couldn't put one past the Islander goalie. Then a few minutes later Isles Ray Ferraro gobbled up a loose puck and headed down the ice on a two on one. At the last second he slid a pass to David Volek who blasted it past Tom Barrasso. The goal at 5:16 stunned the Penguins faithful and abruptly ended Pittsburgh's season. Silence and sadness filled the Civic Arena as everyone realized there would be no third consecutive Stanley Cup.

Did you know the New York Islanders have never won a playoff series since this one?

180) July 31

Wrestlers pound each other under open skies

Over 7,000 fans came out to see some of the best wrestlers/entertainers in the business. In total 7 matches were contested that night. The results were: 1) Damian defeated Damian Demento, 2) The 1-2-3 Kid took care of Rick Martel. 3) WWF IC Champion Shawn Michaels disposed of Mr. Perfect. 4) Jerry Lawlor beat Randy Savage via disqualification when Bret Hart interfered. 5) The Bushwhackers and Tiger Jackson teamed up for a victory over Blake Beverly, the Brooklyn Brawler and Little Louie. 6) Doink the Clown pinned Marty Jannetty and 7) Bret Hart defeated Mr. Hughes.

In addition to the colorful characters in the ring, fans that came out that night got a rare treat. For the first time in more than 2 years the roof of the Civic Arena was opened! So not only did some of the wrestlers see stars but also audience members.

181) September 19

This thing has "Mass" appeal!

As part of its 150th Anniversary in Pittsburgh, the Catholic Diocese celebrated a special Mass at the Civic Arena. Bishop Wuerl (now Bishop of Washington D.C.) was the presider to the estimated crowd of 10,000 celebrants. One of the guests was Archbishop Agostino Cacciavillan, apostolic pronuncio-the pope's personal representative to the United States. At one point he stated "I have seen many of these functions, and this is really one of the best. The Civic Arena has become a temple."

One of the highlights of the Mass came at the beginning. A procession headed by two teenage girls Mary Marasti and Jamie Frank proceeded to the altar. Both carried terra cotta bowls of incense which infused the whole arena. Following close behind were a variety of people representing ethnic groups and organizations. Among them were nuns. Finally a host of priests then bishops completed the formation. As they all walked forward, a 200-voice choir sang the entrance hymn. What a start to a faith-filled event!

Another interesting part of this Mass came with the reading of the gospels. They were read in Greek, Latin, English and Spanish representing the older and newer languages of the church.

Did you know The Mass represented the final event to the yearlong celebration of the Catholic Diocese in Pittsburgh?

182) October 8

"Frank"ly I think this was a family affair!

The 77 year-old Frank Sinatra brought back a lot of memories on this night. Unfortunately this was the last time "Ol Blue Eyes" played a concert at the Civic Arena.

The show started with an opening act but it was not a musical one. Comedian Don Rickles got the crowd going with his usual brash humor. Later Frank hit the stage but seemed a bit moody. He had a complaint about the lack of good song writers and struggled somewhat with a couple of words from songs despite the huge tele-prompters in front of him. As he got further into his show his voice and mood got better. His set list included favorites like: Nelson Riddle's I've Got You Under My Skin, Fly Me To The Moon, Strangers In The Night, Luck Be A Lady, Mack The Knife, My Way, and (Theme of) New York, New York.

The orchestra that night was conducted by Frank's son Frank Sinatra Jr. and included jazz guitarist Ron Anthony from Homewood (Pittsburgh).

Did you know Frank Sinatra who was also known as "Chairman of the Board" passed away on May 14, 1998 at the age of 82?

183) October 29

The NBA Champs pay a visit

On this day Pittsburgh basketball fans got to see the NBA champs Chicago Bulls as they came to town for a pre-season game. Many of the nearly sold-out crowd (16,655) had purchased tickets months in advance hoping to see their hero Michael Jordan. Unfortunately 3 weeks before the game (October 6) Jordan announced his retirement. The three-time NBA champ called it a career at the ripe old age of 30.

Despite Jordan's absence Chicago played well and beat the Philadelphia 76's 110 to 94, however for many Bulls and basketball fans there was something missing. For the record B.J. Armstrong led Chicago with 27 points.

Did you know before returning to the Bulls in 1995 Michael Jordan tried to become a professional baseball player?

184) December 20

Panthers get "Tar" feathered

In men's basketball the North Carolina Tar Heels defeated the Pittsburgh Panthers 106-93. The record sellout crowd (the largest to date to witness a sporting event at the Civic Arena) of 17,716 and the nationally televised audience saw how the # 2 ranked and defending NCAA champions Tar Heels were too much for the Panthers on this night.

Pittsburgh started the game well with an 8 to 0 score. The Tar Heels finally found their rhythm and came back with a 47 to 45 lead at half-time. North

Carolina continued to click in the second half as their inside game reached another gear. They went on a 23-8 run that literally put the game out of reach. Pittsburgh made the score a little more respectable at the end of the fourth quarter but it was too little too late. The Tar Heels were lead by Donald Williams (Most Outstanding Player in the Final Four last season) with 24 points, Jerry Stackhouse (the nation's top schoolboy the season before) with 17 and Eric Montross with 15 points and 9 rebounds. The Tar Heels were blessed with 3 seven-footers on their squad and they all had skill.

Did you know former Blackhawk High School (Pittsburgh) graduate Dante Calabria was also a member of the Tar Heels?

1994

185) March 12

What's in a name?

In the category of bizarre names, Doink and Dink the Clown defeated Bam Bam Bigelow and Luna Vachon in women's professional wrestling (WWF). Doink pinned Bigelow with a school boy drop roll after distraction from Dink.

In the men's matches that night, the Bushwackers defeated Well Dunn with the Battering Ram, WWT Tag Team Champions the Quebecers took care of the 1-2-3 Kid and Jim Powers (Substitute for Marty Jannetty) following the Tower of Quebec, the Smoking Gunns beat Samu and Afa (substitute for Fatu) following the Sidewinder, WWF Champion Yokozuna and Bastion Booger disposed of Men on a Mission when Yoko pinned Mo with a leg drop while Bret Hart and Lex Luger defeated Owen Hart (Bret's younger brother) and IRS when Luger pinned IRS with the running forearm.

Did you know Owen Hart died in 1999 in a real-life accident at the WWE pay-per-view event "Over the Edge" in Kansas City, Missouri? The Canadian wrestler was only 34 years old.

186) April 5

Sin bin shenanigans!

The Pittsburgh Penguins defeated the Tampa Bay Lightning 2-1 in a bizarre night for Mario Lemieux. Usually Lemieux got headlines for his scoring prowess but this game was different. It started when Lemieux was hooked twice (including once in the face) late in the first period. Unfortunately the referees didn't see the infractions so no penalties were called. Soon after Mario high-sticked Tampa's Roman Hamrlik and was sent to the sin bin for 2 minutes. Visibly upset when he sat down, Mario threw his stick onto the ice. Apparently Lemieux claimed his stick was broken and needed a new one anyways. Meanwhile linesman Jerry Pateman gave Mario his old stick back while referee Terry Fraser assessed Mario a10-minute misconduct for his display. Lemieux was furious over the call and stormed out of the penalty box. He chased Fraser looking to injure him. Just before getting to his target he was intercepted by teammates Ron Francis, Ulf Samuelsson and Kjell Samuelsson. The three of them held Lemieux back and tried to calm him down. Fraser had seen enough and kicked Mario out of the contest (game misconduct). As the superstar left the ice surface he received a rousing applause.

Did you know after this incident Lemieux was fined $500.00 by the NHL? Mario was saved from suspension because he had no previous history nor did he actually hit referee Terry Fraser.

187) June 12

Sharks get sand kicked in their face!

Were you there when the Pittsburgh Stingers defeated the Arizona Sandsharks 10-4? This was the Stingers debut in the Major Continental Soccer League. On this opening night, 5,917 spectators got to see indoor soccer played outdoors- the retractable roof was opened for this occasion. The game was also important because it marked the return of professional soccer to Pittsburgh. The Pittsburgh Spirit was the first team to play in town but they folded after the 1986 season.

The Pittsburgh Stingers were coached by former British star Paul Child and featured both international and local players. Kia (Iran) led the Stingers this night with 3 goals and 1 assist while Doug Petras (Robert Morris College by way of Norwin High) put in a solid goal tending performance. Fans also saw home town boys Dave Kasper (Chartiers Valley High) and Peter Smith (Upper St. Clair) on the Pittsburgh team.

Did you know during this home opener, the public address system played "Flight of the Bumble Bee" during Stinger power plays? Also the P.A. announcer called goalkeeper Doug Petras the Beekeeper.

188) June 18

Phantoms have ants in their pants?

In hockey of a different kind, the Pittsburgh Phantoms thrilled fans by beating the Atlanta Fire Ants 10-9 in a shoot-out. This game marked the Civic Arena debut of the Phantoms in the Roller Hockey International league. More than 7,300 people attended the closely contested game.

Some notable players for the Phantoms included former Penguins like: Alain Lemieux (older brother of Mario), Brian Trottier (who only played home games for the Phantoms) and Warren Young. Young was also assistant coach while ex-Penguin Rick Kehoe was the head coach. Another member of the team was local product Jamie Adams. Adams was the only hockey player from Shaler area high school to have his number retired. The feisty player who didn't mind roughing things up received a game misconduct on this night.

Did you know the Phantoms would accumulate a home record of 9 wins and 2 losses-good enough to qualify for the post season? They won their first round play-off series against the Chicago Cheetahs with a combined score of 31 to 15 but then lost to the Minnesota Arctic Blast in the second round. Unfortunately after their initial season the Phantoms folded or more appropriately "disappeared".

189) August 25

Pittsburgh survives arctic blast!

In roller hockey action the Pittsburgh Phantoms blanketed the Minnesota Arctic Blast 8-6 in the first game of the second round of the play-offs. During the game the Civic Arena roof opened to the Space Odyssey theme song. This was the first and only time the stainless steel dome was open for a professional hockey game-albeit a roller hockey one!

Did you know the Phantoms got their name from the "Steel Phantom" a roller coaster at Kennywood Park in West Mifflin, Pennsylvania?

190) September 11

Dallas' Doyle does double duty

Were you there when the Dallas Sidekicks defeated the Pittsburgh Stingers 5-3 in play-off soccer action? This game officially eliminated the Stingers from the quarter finals in their inaugural season. The Stingers had been "kicked around" in their first game in Dallas by an embarrassing 15 to 3 shellacking!

Did you know David Doyle a forward for Dallas and third-leading scorer in the CISL during the regular season was forced to play goalkeeper in the second half of this game? Regular Sidekick goalie Hank Henry sprained his right knee when he collided with Stingers' Chris Kelly. The attendance that night was 3,106.

191) October 1

That was a "Damme" good deal

The Pittsburgh Penguins played their IHL farm team the Cleveland Lumberjacks as part of the shooting for the movie Sudden Death starring Jean Claude Van Damme. The contest was supposed to represent Game 7 of the Stanley Cup Finals with the Lumberjacks playing the role of the Chicago Blackhawks.

Not all players from the Penguins participated in the game though former NHL'ers Luc Robitaille, Markus Naslund, Jay Caufield and Ian Moran did. Caufield actually played Pens goalie Brad Tolliver while teammate Robitaille scored the tying goal on a breakaway that forced "sudden death" overtime. Pens' Ian Moran dressed for the Lumberjacks and represented Chicago Blackhawk defenseman Chris Chelios.

Pat Brisson a former player from the Quebec Major Junior Hockey League and current NHL agent also played in the game. Brisson counts present Penguin players Sidney Crosby and Evgeni Malkin among his biggest clients.

Sudden Death film makers enticed fans to come to watch the mock hockey game by offering them free: admission, food and parking. Ten thousand people took up the offer! To make up for some of the other 7,000 empty seats at the Civic Arena, cardboard cut outs of spectators were used.

The producer of Sudden Death was Howard Baldwin-then owner of the Pittsburgh Penguins. His wife Karen Elise Baldwin wrote the movie but also played a TV director in the film. The Pittsburgh Penguins were not playing regular pre-season games at this time due to the labor dispute between NHL owners and players.

Did you know the game between the Pittsburgh Penguins and their farm team the Cleveland Lumberjacks did not provide enough realistic footage for the film? Thus scenes from the game did not make final production.

192) October 11

Pavarotti plays for Pittsburgh

Were you there when the legendary Luciano Pavarotti gave a concert for his faithful followers? The rotund Italian tenor delighted the Civic Arena audience with a repertory of songs such as: "Quando le sere", "O Paradiso", "Matinatta", "Non ti scordar di me" and "Girometta" and arias such as: "I Lombardi", "Werther", "Tosca" and "I Pagliacci". On this night the eve of Pavarotti's 59th birthday 9,000 fans paid up to $195.00 to see him perform.

Pavarotti dedicated the song "Girometta" to Pittsburgh teacher and singer Claudia Pinza? She was in the audience and had told Pavarotti that it was a favorite song of her father, the great basso Ezio Pinza.

Unfortunately for music and opera lovers around the world, Pavarotti passed away on September 6, 2007 from pancreatic cancer? He was 71 years old.

193) October 27-30

Blades of glory

On these days the Civic Arena hosted Skate America International. Fans got to see the best male and female skaters from around the world. The medal winners were the following: Women's singles, gold = Surya Bonaly (France), silver = Michele Kwan (U.S.) and bronze = Irina Slutskaya (Russia). For the men's singles, gold = Todd Eldredge (U.S.), silver = Philippe Candeloro (France) and bronze = Eric Millot (France).

In Ice Dancing, gold = Liz Punsalen and Jerod Swallow (U.S.), silver = Marina Anissina (Russian born) and Gwendal Peizerat (France) and bronze = Elizaveta Sketolnikova and Dmitri Kazalig (Kazakhstan).

In the Pairs, gold = Marina Eltsova and Andrei Buskov (Russia), silver = Evgenia Shiskova and Vadim Naumov (Russia) and bronze Radka Kovarikova and Rene Novotny (Czech Republic).

One of the more interesting moments of the ice dancing competition came during the long program of Punsalen and Swallow. A stirrup strap on Swallow's right skate broke and caused him to trip and fall head first to the ice. After the mishap and some discussion amongst the judges Swallow and his partner (who was also his wife) were able to re-start their 4.5 minute routine. This time they skated without incident and went on to capture the gold medal for the U.S. Ironically at the 1994 Winter Olympics in Lillehammer Swallow dropped Punsalen after stepping on a metal bolt. Unfortunately the judges at that time were not as generous so no re-start was awarded.

Though the caliber of skaters was high for Skate America International organizers were disappointed that only 21,000 people showed up for the 4-day event.

Did you know during the gala exhibition (which was the final non-judging session of the Skate America International) skater Phillippe Candeloro jumped over the boards and landed in the lap of 21 year-old Anne Bradel? She was surprised but delighted. Soon afterwards a horde of women came rushing to the area hoping to get a piece of the flamboyant Frenchman.

1995

194) January 17

The retractable roof meets a sudden death

The Wheeling Thunderbirds (now called Nailers) and the Johnstown Chiefs, two hockey teams in the East Coast Hockey League served as stunt doubles for the Chicago Blackhawks and the Pittsburgh Penguins respectively in an exhibition game for the movie "Sudden Death".

In the film, during Game 7 of the Stanley Cup Finals the Vice President of the United States was held hostage inside a luxury suite by terrorists. Jean Claude Van Damme who played Darren McCord tried to rescue the Vice President but had to do it before the end of the game or else the arena would be blown up.

One of the strange scenes in the film came during this hockey game. High above the action the Civic Arena roof opened up but everyone seemed oblivious to it!

Did you know after the filming of "Sudden Death" a new scoreboard was installed in the Civic Arena? Though it was great addition for the building it made it more difficult for the retractable roof to be fully opened.

195) February 7

This was not your average "Joe"

Were you there when thirty-seven year-old Joe Mullen of the Penguins became the first American born player to obtain 1000 career points in the NHL? He reached the milestone 28 seconds into the second period with an assist. The crowd of 11,131, the smallest since November 1, 1988 gave him a standing ovation.

Mullen became the 42nd NHL player to hit the 1000 point mark. He finished the game with 2 goals and 2 assists while his Penguins beat the Florida Panthers 7-3.

Did you know Joe Mullen was also the first American born player to score 500 career goals? He ended his career with over 1500 points.

196) March 25

Page and Plant produce record

As part of their "Unledded Tour" Jimmy Page and Robert Plant brought their high energy show to the 'Burgh. Opening with The Wanton Song and Bring It On Home, the former Led Zeppelin greats continued to rock the Pittsburgh crowd all night. With fresh twists to old standards like the Egyptian flavored rendition of Kashmir to the hurdy-gurdy feel of Nobody's Fault But Mine, the songs felt new and inspired.

Added to the musical range and diversity that night was: ex-Cure guitarist Porl Thompson, mandolin player Jim Sutherland, keyboardist Ed Shearmur, singer Najma Akhtar and a host of symphony musicians. The 17,764 spectators who came out also broke an attendance record for a rock show at the Civic Arena.

Did you know the opening act for this concert was Pittsburgh's own Rusted Root? They had the crowd pumped up and some even dancing with songs like: Send Me On My Way, Lost in the Crowd, Martyr and Ecstasy.

197) April 29

A symphony of stars

On this bright night the Civic Arena presented a "Night of Two Thousand Stars". Two thousand lucky Pennsylvania music students got to perform with the Pittsburgh Symphony led by conductor Lorin Maazel. The students came from 36 area high school choirs and were joined by the 1995 Pennsylvania High School All-State Orchestra and Chorus and the Kiski Area High School Marching Band.

The students with the Symphony performed classics such as "Ode to Joy" from Beethoven's Ninth Symphony and Tchaikovsky's "1812 Overture". They also honored the late Henry Mancini (Pittsburgh) with musical pieces such as Moon River, Baby Elephant Walk, The Pink Panther and Peter Gunn.

After the show, audience members and performers got a special treat. The roof was opened for a firework display. According to my research this may have been the last time the dome was retracted.

Did you know the Kiski Area High School Marching Band won the 1991 and 1994 Class AA National Championships of Bands of America? They were directed by George Wozniak.

198) August 20

Precki picks Pittsburgh apart

Were you there when the San Jose Grizzlies tamed the Pittsburgh Stingers 13-7 in Major Continental Soccer League action? Stan Precki (Predrag Radosavljevic) of the Grizzlies put on an offensive display when he scored 3 goals and collected 6 assists for a 9-point night! For the superstar Precki this was just another day at the office as this was his 8th hat trick of the season.

Did you know the Yugoslavian born Precki had 351 goals and 352 assists in 360 indoor games up to this point?

199) August 27

Civic slams a record

The WWF Summer Slam played to an audience of 18,062 which to date was the largest crowd to see any event at the Pittsburgh Civic Arena. Some highlights of this 8th annual pay-per-view event were: Hakushi beat the 1-2-3 Kid, Hunter Hearst Hemsley pinned Bob Holly after a Pedigree, The Smokin' Gunns downed the Blu Brothers, Barry Horowitz took care of Skip with a roll-up, The Undertaker slammed the door shut on Kama in a Casket Match, Bret Hart won by disqualification over Isaac Yankem, Shawn Michaels retained the WWF Intercontinental Championship when he disposed of Razor Ramon, Diesel pinned King Mabel after a Flying Clothesline and kept his WWF Championship while Bertha Faye (with Harvey Wippleman) defeated Alundra Blayze to win the WWF Women's Championship.

Did you know this was the only time that the WWF Women's Championship changed hands at a SummerSlam event?

200) September 17

Give peace a chance

Were you there for the Walk For Peace fund-raiser? It was put together by Cathy Howe, wife and mother of three from South Hills, Pittsburgh. Howe had visited Medjugorje, Bosnia as part of a humanitarian group in June 1994 after the Bosnian War. She was awestruck by the plight of the refugees and upon returning to Pittsburgh helped organize (with the help of Penguin star Jaromir Jagr-native of the Czech Republic) a WALK FOR PEACE at the Pittsburgh Civic Arena. The walk helped raise awareness and money for Bosnian orphans.

Later Cathy Howe continued her charitable ways and started a Foundation called Mother's Hope which helps sick and disadvantaged children here and abroad.

Did you know Cathy Howe's brother-in-law is former Penguin star Pierre Larouche?

201) September 29-October 31

Be afraid! Be very afraid!

Robert Short's "Terrordome" shook up the Civic Arena for over a month. This haunted house Halloween type freak show filled the bowels of the Civic Arena. Live and near live creepy and scary actors taunted and spooked spectators in corridors and special rooms located below the arena ice level. The special effects combined with horrific movie sets were so frightening that one customer actually passed out! Thankfully she was okay after being revived.

Did you know Robert Short has been involved in such movies as Beetlejuice, E.T., Addams Family Values, Splash, Lethal Weapon 4 and The Predator among many others?

202) November 29

Dukes double dribble with Panthers

The Pittsburgh Panthers men's basketball team defeated Duquesne 84-73 thus ruining Scott Edgar's debut as the Dukes new coach. The game was a sloppy affair especially in the first half. Pittsburgh committed 18 turnovers while Duquesne had 13. Duquesne employed a trapping press to slow down the Panthers but it only partially worked. Pittsburgh scored the first 10 points of the game and held on for the victory. They were led by Freshman Vonteego Cummings with 18 points, 8 rebounds, 4 assists and 1 steal. The Dukes' Tom Pipkins with 27 points was the high man of the game while teammate Nick Bosnic had 22 and 10 rebounds.

Earlier on the same evening, the Duquesne Dukes women's basketball team beat the lady Panthers 55-53 in a nail biter. The game was decided with only 3.9 seconds left on the clock as Duquesne's Trixie Wolf converted a pass from All-American Korie Hlede. Initially Hlede looked like she was going to shoot as she drove the lane but then dished it off to Wolf for an easy lay-up and a victory for the lady Dukes.

This was a rare double-header for the city basketball teams at the Civic Arena. Officials from both schools saw it as a way to boost attendance. It must have worked-11,489 fans showed up!

Did you know there have only been 2 other double-headers between Pittsburgh and Duquesne? They happened in 1996 and 1998.

203) December 27

There's something new about Antigua!

The Harlem Globetrotters played a zany basketball game against the International All-Stars. Though the Globetrotters had performed at the Civic Arena many times, this night was special for two reasons. First, it featured the debut of 6'7" Orlando Antigua-the only non-black player to play for the storied Globetrotter team since 1943. Secondly, Antigua had played for the Pittsburgh Panthers from 1991-1995 so area basketball fans were quite familiar with him. In his 4-year career at the university he scored 903 points.

Antigua played for the Harlem Globetrotters until 2002 and then took various assistant coaching jobs in Pittsburgh and elsewhere. He currently lives in Lexington where he is assistant coach at the University of Kentucky.

Did you know on Halloween Night 1988 Orlando Antigua (then still a teenager) was shot in the head in a drive-by shooting? Apparently the bullet lodged on the side of his head but was never removed because doctors feared it was too close to the brain. Antigua finally had it removed in 1994 when he complained of earaches. Doctors found the bullet in his ear canal.

1991

168. http://hockey.ballparks.com/NHL/PittsburghPenguins/index.htm

168. bobgaineyenwikipedia.org

169. Pittsburgh Post-Gazette, August 3, 1991, Page Number B2

169. Pittsburgh Post-Gazette, August 10, 1991, Page Number B2

170. en.wikipedia.org/wiki/1991_Canada_Cup.

170. Observer-Reporter. Washington, Pennsylvania, September 1, 1991

171. www.letsgopens.com/penshist.htm

171. www.pensinfo.com/3q=node/358

171. denver.yourhub.com/Englewood/Stories/Sports/general-Sports/Story~323843.aspx

1992

172. The Valley Independent, April 4, 1992

172. Pittsburgh Post-Gazette, April 1, 1992 D2

172. Pittsburgh Post-Gazette, April 4, 1992 C3

173. query.nytimes.com/gst/fullpage.html?res=9E0CE1DC1E3DF937A15757C0A964958260

174. Pittsburgh Post-Gazette, May 27, 1992

175. Pittsburgh Post-Gazette, August 14, 1992

175. The Valley Independent, August 20, 1992

176. query.nytimes.com/gst/fullpage.htm?res=9D0CE6DA163FF93BA25753C1A967958260

1993

177. http://www.databasehockey.com/teams/teamscores.htm?m=PIT&yr=1992

178. http://www.theagitator.com/2003/02/27/its-a-sad-day-in-the-neighborhood/

178. http://www.theagitator.com/archives/004905.php

178. Pittsburgh Post-Gazette, May 2, 1992

179. Pittsburgh Post-Gazette, May 15, 1993

180. http://www.angelfire.com/wrestling/cawthon777/93.htm

181. Pittsburgh Post-Gazette, September 20, 1993 Page Number B-1

182. Pittsburgh Post-Gazette, October 9, 1993 Page Number 27

183. Pittsburgh Post-Gazette, October 30, 1993

184. Pittsburgh Post-Gazette, December 21, 1993, Page Number D-1

1994

185. www.lethalwow.com/history/1994wwfmatches

185. www.thehistoryofwwe.com/94.htm

186. http://mystic.verizon.net/vze7mp9/id20.html

187. Pittsburgh Post-Gazette, June 13, 1994 Page Number D-3

188. Pittsburgh Post-Gazette, June 19, 1994 Page Number C-4

189. http://www.pittsburghhockey.net/Common/CivicArena/CivicArena.html

189. Pittsburgh Post-Gazette, August 26, 1994 Page Number B-3

190. Pittsburgh Post-Gazette, September 12, 1994 Page Number D-10

191. Pittsburgh Post-Gazette, October 1&2, 1994 Page Number B-1

191. Pittsburghhockey.net/Common/Civic Arena/Suddendeath.html

192. Pittsburgh Post-Gazette, October 12, 1994 Page Number A-1

192. http://en.wikipedia.org/wiki/Luciano_Pavarotti

193. Pittsburgh Post-Gazette, October 31, 1994 Page Number D-2

193. en.wikipedia.org/wiki/Skate_America

1995

194. Pittsburgh Post-Gazette, January 17, 1995 Page Number D-8

194. http://www.funtrivia.com/submitquiz.cfm?quiz=262490

195. Pittsburgh Post-Gazette, February 8, 1995 Page Number D-1

195. findarticles.com/p/articles/mi_m0FCM/is_7_30/ai_84394820/pg_3

196. http://chicago.citysearch.com/profile/11278515

197. Pittsburgh Post-Gazette, April 28, 1995 Page Number 6

197. Pittsburgh Post Gazette, May 5, 1995 Page Number 31

198. Pittsburgh Post-Gazette, August 21, 1995 Page Number D-4

199. http://www.prowrestlinghistory.com/supercards/usa/wwf/summer.html

199. SlummerSlam1995-ProWrestlingWiki

200. www.blacktie-pittsburgh.com/premiere_events/details.cfm?id=62

201. Pittsburgh Post-Gazette, September 29 &October 27, 1995 Page Number 3

202. Pittsburgh Post-Gazette, November 30, 1995 Page Number C-1&C-3

203. Pittsburgh Post-Gazette, December 27, 1995 D-6

Chapter 8, 1996-2000

1996

<u>204) February 23</u>

A couple Penguins have a whale of a time!

Two Penguins reached seasonal milestones when Pittsburgh defeated the Hartford Whalers 5-4. Superstars Mario Lemieux and Jaromir Jagr both scored their 50th goals of the season. Each player came into the game 2 goals shy of the magic number. Lemieux got his 49th goal in the first period while Jagr got his 49th in the second period. Both got their 50th in the third period. On the losing end, Whaler forward Brendan Shanahan had 3 goals and 1 assist for Hartford.

In the 1995-96 NHL season Mario Lemieux and Jaromir Jagr finished first and second respectively in the scoring race.

Did you know Mario Lemieux became the first player in the NHL to get 50 goals this year? The goal was also significant because it gave him 544 career goals tying him with the legendary Maurice "The Rocket" Richard. Meanwhile Jaromir Jagr became the first Czech born player to score 50 goals in an NHL season.

205) March 26

Lemieux makes St. Louis feel a little blue

With a standing room only crowd the Pittsburgh Penguins embarrassed the St. Louis Blues 8-4. In a dazzling offensive display Mario Lemieux scored 5 goals and collected 2 assists for a 7-point night. This was the last time "Super Mario" faced Wayne Gretzky at the Civic Arena. Gretzky ended the night with 1 assist.

Up to this point in their NHL careers Gretzky and Lemieux faced each other 21 times. Gretzky had 51 points in these games while Lemieux had 37.

If you were at the Pens/Blues game you might recall what happened to Shayne Corson. The Blues forward suffered a concussion and broken jaw when J.J. Daigneault hit him into the boards three minutes into the contest.

Did you know two days before this game Mario Lemieux's first son Austin Nicholas was born 3 months prematurely? He weighed only 2 pounds 6 ounces.

206) March 31

I'm lovin' it!

In the 19th edition of the McDonald's All-American Game the East defeated the West 120-105. One of the highlights of this annual high school basketball classic included 27 dunks. Though both teams scored some spectacular baskets the game also produced 65 turnovers. At halftime the score was evened at 55 but the East opened it up in the third quarter with a 20-3 run.

The East's Shaheen Holloway (Elizabeth, New Jersey) won the MVP award with 7 points, 8 assists and 6 steals. Other scorers for the East were Stephen Jackson (Port Arthur, Texas) with 21 to lead the team, Vassil Evtimov (Bulgaria) with 14 points and 11 rebounds and Kobe Bryant (Philadelphia, PA) with 13 points and 3 assists. For the West Winfred Walton (Detroit, Michigan) had 21 points and 7 rebounds off the bench while Corey Benjamin (Compton California) had 17 points. The attendance was 13,411.

Did you know Kobe Bryant's father Joe "Jellybean" Bryant played for Team Pennsylvania in the 8th annual Dapper Dan Roundball Classic held on April 7, 1972 at the Civic Arena? He received the MVP award.

207) October 6

Pittsburgh flips over Olympic heroes

Were you there for the Tour of World and Olympic Gymnasts/the 1996-1997 Magnificent 7 Tour? Members of the 1996 USA Women's Gold Medal Gymnastics team competed against gymnasts from various countries around the world. For the American girls the tour gave them a chance to showcase their talents to a larger audience. The Magnificent 7 were: Shannon Miller, Amanda Borden, Amy Chow, Jaycie Phelps, Dominique Moceanu, Dominique Dawes and Kerri Strug. Unfortunately Strug did not appear due to injuries sustained at the Olympics. The gymnasts also came back to Pittsburgh on November 30, 1997-the last date of the tour.

Did you know the 1996 Summer Olympics were held in Atlanta from July 19 to August 9th?

1997

208) February 4

Lemieux joins an elite club

On this night the Pittsburgh Penguins got by the Vancouver Canucks 6-4. Mario Lemieux scored his 600th career goal when he put the puck into an empty net with 51 seconds left in the game. The sold-out crowd of 17,355 recognized his accomplishment and gave him a standing ovation. Lemieux became the second fastest NHL player to reach this goal total (only Wayne Gretzky did it in less games-one less to be exact).

Did you know to this point only 6 other NHL players had scored 600 goals or more? They were the following: Wayne "The Great One" Gretzky, Mr. Hockey" Gordie Howe, Marcel Dionne, Phil Esposito, Mike Gartner and Bobby "The Golden Jet" Hull.

209) March 14

March Madness hits the 'Burgh

Were you there when Louisville (No. 6) defeated Massachusetts (No. 11) 65-57, New Mexico (No. 3) got by Old Dominion 59-55 (No. 14), Texas (No.10) beat Wisconsin 71-58 (No.7) and Coppin State (No 15) surprised

South Carolina 78-65 (No 2) in the Regional of the men's NCAA basketball championships?

Coppin State, a small school in Baltimore, Maryland pulled off the biggest first round upset in tournament history winning by 13 points. They also became the first Mid-Eastern Atlantic Conference team to win a game in the March Madness. To date only 2 other No. 15 ranked schools won a tournament game.

A record college basketball crowd of 17, 509 cheered on Coppin State with "Let's Go Eagles, Let's Go Eagles" louder and louder as victory seemed inevitable for the underdog team. When the final buzzer sounded the place exploded. Not bad for a team who were down by 7 points at one point in the second half!

Did you know earlier on that same day, the Coppin State players had booked out of their hotel rooms thinking they would never be back to play a second game? Also the team had borrowed a band, Morgan State (their rival in Baltimore) to help with cheering and had a substitute mascot take over in the second half. It seems the first one sprained his ankle playing with the Texas one.

210) March 16

Respect for an underdog

In a squeaker Louisville defeated New Mexico 64-63 in men's NCAA second round basketball action. In the next game little Coppin State (No. 15) almost pulled off the impossible again but finally lost in a thriller to Texas. The players on Coppin State were cheered before and during the game as the 17,500 fans wanted another upset. Just 2 days before the Eagles knocked off No.2 South Carolina in a game for the ages.

Down by 10 points at the half (49-39) against Texas, Coppin State mounted a memorable comeback. Led by the skinny 6-2 Antoine Brockington, the Eagles outscored the Longhorns early in the third period. Then Brockington brought the crowd to its feet when he drained a 3-pointer to give his team a 53-50 lead. Coppin State stymied Longhorns star Reggie Freeman for awhile but the All-American finally got on track and drained 15 points in a 6-minute stretch. Down by 8 points this time the Eagles once again dug deep. With 42 seconds left on the clock Brockington dropped another 3-pointer and his game high 27th point and Coppin State were only down by 1. The Longhorns tried to get the next basket but an intercepted errant pass with less than 20 seconds left gave the Eagles hope for another upset. Then with 5 seconds left Coppin's

Danny Singletary went in for a layup but Freeman swatted it out of bounds. The Eagles while rejected still had an ounce of hope. As they attempted an inbound pass for a last second play it was intercepted by Longhorns DeJuan Vasquez. The buzzer sounded and the impossible dream died. Texas won the nail-biter 82-81.

211) April 19

The pretty Colleens can dance!

The Lord of The Dance took their breath away. Civic Arena audiences of all ages got to see the phenomenon that swept the world from the mid 1990's. Thirty-eight year old Michael Flatley and company demonstrated speed and precision as they pumped up the traditional Irish dance to new heights. Combined with spectacular lighting, music and color it turned out to be a feast for the senses.

The Lord of The Dance actually performed twice this day and 30,000 people came out for it. The show produced 3 encores.

Did you know Michael Flatley was born in Chicago and at the age of 11became the first non-European resident to win the All-Ireland World Championship for Irish dance?

212) June 16

That's a high price for success!

On this day the Civic Arena hosted a "Personal Success Seminar." The 2,300 attendees, who included business owners, college students, sales represen-tatives, health care professionals and retirees, paid up to $250.00 to hear stories and professional advice from 10 special guests. They were: General Colin Powell, former first lady Barbara Bush, NBC news anchor Tom Brokaw, busi-nessman and author Harvey MacKay, former Steeler Lynn Swann, Heather Whitestone McCallum, the first hearing impaired woman to win the Miss America title, Oprah's fitness guru Bob Greene, personal finance columnist Jane Bryant Quinn, entrepreneur Frank Meeks and negotiator extraordinaire, Herb Cohen. The speakers touched on a host of themes like; working hard, developing talents, studying, treating others fairly and trust in God.

Harvey Mackay promoted his new book called "Dig Your Well Before You're Thirsty" which addressed networking strategies for the 21st century. Two of his other books, "Swim With the Sharks Without Being Eaten Alive" and "Beware of the Naked Man Who Offers You His Shirt" were both best-sellers. Before his appearance in Pittsburgh Mackay was quoted, "I believe our lives change in two ways. It's the people we meet and the books we read..."

213) June 21

Is there a draft in the room?

Were you there when the Civic Arena hosted the National Hockey League (NHL) Entry Draft? This was the first and only time the draft was held in the city of Pittsburgh. Two-hundred and forty-six players were selected in nine rounds. The top ten chosen and their teams were 1) Joe Thorton (Boston), 2) Patrick Marleau (San Jose), 3) Olli Jokinen (Los Angeles), 4) Roberto Luongo (NY Islanders), 5) Eric Brewer (NY Islanders), 6) Daniel Tkaczuk (Calgary), 7) Paul Mara (Tampa Bay), 8) Sergei Samsonov (Boston), 9) Nick Boyton (Washington) and 10) Brad Ference (Vancouver).

The Pittsburgh Penguins drafted nine players in the following order: 1) Slovakian Robert Dome (17th), 2) Brian Gaffaney (44th), 3) Josef Melichar (71st), 4) Alexander Mathieu (97th), 5) Harlan Pratt (124th), 6) Petr Havelka (152nd), 7) Mark Moore (179th), 8) Andrew Ference (208th) and Eric Lind (234th). None of the Penguin draftees are currently playing for the team.

One player drafted this year and 12th overall by the Ottawa Senators was ex-Penguin Marian Hossa. Most fans will remember him for jumping ship after the 2008 Stanley Cup Finals loss. The next year he lost in the Finals again as a member of the Detroit Red Wings when Pittsburgh got revenge.

Did you know a month before the NHL Draft 9,000 free tickets were given away for the event?

214) July 14

These kids ACT-SO well!

The National Association for the Advancement of Colored People's (NAACP's) 19th annual Afro-Academic, Cultural, Technological and Scientific Olympics (ACT-SO) competition was held this day. Over 800 students (9th to 12th graders) from across the U.S. performed various academic and artistic activities (i.e. dancing and singing). Overall, 72 youngsters received honors for their achievements.

Did you know actors T.C. Carlson and Crystal Fox hosted this competition which was videotaped by Chicago-based Central City Production? Among the 2,000 audience members were: boxing promoter Don King, San Francisco mayor Willie Brown and Pittsburgh Mayor Tom Murphy.

215) August 1-2

Support for the soul

Were you there for The Women of Faith- "Joyful Journey" Conference in Pittsburgh? Over 16,000 women gathered at the Civic Arena to celebrate their faith. Like Promise Keepers for men (yet not the same organization) these women of all ages and Christian denominations came together to discuss, support and rejuvenate their spirits.

Some of the speakers this day included: humorist Barbara Johnson founder of the Spatula Ministries, television host Thelma Wells and Patsy Claimont author of such books as, God Uses Cracked Pots and Normal Is Just A Setting on Your Dryer.

216) October 13-18

Greene County goes great with Garth!

Garth Brooks dazzled Pittsburgh concert goers with six sold-out shows! Over 100,000 people came to see one of the most popular country singers in the 1990's.

The 35-year old Brooks started with a bang on opening night when he rose from below the stage with a white piano. The music then took over and fans were hooked. Some of the highlights included: the sing-a-long of Friends in Low Places, the perfect blend of rock 'n' roll and country as the band played American Honky-Tonk Bar Association, the ballad The Beaches of Cheyenne and the Elvis-the-pelvis thrusts on Shameless.

On his October 17th show Garth got a cheer when he wore a Steelers jersey with the number 1 on it. Earlier that same day Brooks attended a Steelers practice at Three Rivers Stadium and chatted with linebacker and fellow Oklahoman Jason Gildon.

In the audience for his last show (October 18) Brooks invited some special guests. Thirty-seven students from the Greene County Voc-tech culinary arts class had received complimentary tickets. All were acknowledged by Brooks as he entered the stage. How were the students lucky enough to get the tickets? They had catered a lunch for his road crew's trip back to Nashville. The items on the menu included: gourmet hoagies, croissant sandwiches, pasta salad, mineral water and chocolate torte.

Did you know Garth Brooks once signed autographs for 23 consecutive hours? It was at Fan Fair in Nashville, Tennessee in 1996.

217) October 19

Skin flick proves to be cruel trick!

Fans got more than they bargained for when Cheap Trick and Motley Crue with opening acts Live Crew and DJ Larceny came to town. After the warm up act a hardcore pornographic video was shown on the stage screen. Many of the 4,642 attendees actually cheered while others were appalled. Later, Motley's drummer Tommy Lee encouraged the crowd to show their breasts for the camera. Some obliged and one particular girl danced like a stripper. Needless to say, after the concert many complaints were filed. Considering minors were in the crowd it was quite a shocking display. Later, Pittsburgh police and the district's attorney's office investigated the incident and eventually fined Aramark Sports and Entertainment Services $5,000 and suspended their license for one week.

218) November 19

The best calls it a day!

Were you there when Mario Lemieux's # 66 was retired in a half-hour pre-game ceremony at the Civic Arena? It was an emotional night as the greatest player in Penguin history was honored. Family, friends and a standing room only crowd of 17,145 (the first sell-out of the year) celebrated Mario's illustrious accomplishments. Also on hand were many former teammates who presented Lemieux with a five-magnum bottle of cabaret Sauvignon. Penguins' co-owners Howard Baldwin and Roger Marino gave Mario a gold medallion and a $250,000 check for the Mario Lemieux Foundation for cancer research. They also gave Lemieux's parents a cruise while his wife Nathalie received a charm bracelet. His 3 daughters got gold necklaces while son Austin received a plaque. Lemieux thanked everyone including the loyal fans. For some in attendance it was tough seeing Mario call it a career. It was probably even tougher knowing what Mario could have done had he stayed healthy throughout his career. However at the age of 32 with injuries and illness it was enough for now.

For the record, in the hockey game played that night the Penguins tied the Boston Bruins 3-3 in overtime (no shoot-outs back then).

Did you know two nights before his retirement ceremony Lemieux was inducted into the Hockey Hall of Fame in Toronto, Canada? He was one of only of ten players in the NHL for whom the Hall of Fame waived its standard 3-year waiting period.

219) December 10-14

Disney dazzles December crowd!

On these 5 cold Pittsburgh nights Walt Disney's "World on Ice-Aladdin" warmed the hearts of many. As usual, the folks at Disney were able to capture the essence of this 1992 animation classic almost to a tee. Aladdin, Princess Jasmine, The Genie and Jafar never looked as good as they "skated" through their roles. Even Iago the parrot and Abu the monkey were part of the show though not as people.

The performers behind the costumes of Aladdin and Princess Jasmine were actually Canadian figure skaters. In fact, Aladdin played by 33 year-old Jaimee Eggleton was the 1984 National Canadian Junior Champion and participated in the Sarajevo Olympics the same year.

Did you know originally the Civic Arena was scheduled to present Andrew Lloyd Weber's "Starlight Express" on Ice during these dates? However, poor attendance at other venues across the country forced its cancellation halfway through the tour.

1998

220) March 17

"I'm All Shook Up"

"Elvis -The Concert" brought back warm thoughts to his loyal fans. Though "The King" had been dead almost 21 years, on this night he lived on in the hearts and minds of many folks who saw this show. The sparse crowd of 4,000 who paid $25.00 a pop consisted mostly of older women. They wanted a trip down memory lane and from all accounts this spectacle fitted the bill.

For those thinking this show was a typical Elvis impersonator kind of deal, they would have been wrong. No the stage was full with Elvis' original band mates, backup singers called The Sweet Inspirations and a jumbo-screen of "the King" signing his songs from previous concerts. Though the setting seemed a bit surreal, diehard fans ate it up like a peanut butter, banana and bacon sandwich (Elvis sandwich).

Did you know Elvis Presley last performed live at the Pittsburgh Civic Arena on December 31, 1976?

221) March 21

A millennium milestone for a classy guy

The Pittsburgh Penguins defeated their state rivals the Philadelphia Flyers 4-3 but the real story focused on their humble captain, Ron Francis. On this night the classy Pen forward got career assist number 1,000. It came late in the second period while the Pens were on a power play. Francis fed a cross-ice pass to Fredrik Olausson who blasted it past Flyer goalie Ron Hextall. The capacity crowd jumped to their feet and acknowledged the milestone with an extended ovation. Among the 17,145 attendees were: Francis' father, wife, son Michael, sister-in-law and mother-in law. To date Francis became only the 7th player in NHL history to have accomplished this feat.

Did you know Francis played 23 years in the NHL and was inducted into the Hockey Hall of Fame on November 12, 2007 along with other greats Mark Messier, Scott Stevens and Al MacInnis?

222) April 19

Music and Guinness go together quite fine!

The sound of music filled the air tonight. In fact a total of 2,049 musicians from Pittsburgh and the surrounding state high schools came together under one roof. Guided by Mariss Jansens, Pittsburgh Symphony Orchestra Music Director, they became the "World's Largest Orchestra". The young musicians, monitored by Guinness Book of Records, comprised of 961 strings, 458 woodwinds, 410 brass and 220 percussionists. The orchestra was so large it covered the entire Civic Arena floor and part of the A-level seating.

The official song played to break the old record was Michaels Moriczs' Music Forever.

Did you know the previous record for the world's largest orchestra was 2,023? It happened in Wolverhampton, England in 1996. The current record is 6,400 plus members of the Vancouver Symphony Orchestra. It occurred on May 15, 2000 when band students from 160 schools across Canada converged on B.C. Place. Led by director Bramwell Tovey, the young musicians played Beethoven's 9th Symphony for 9 minutes and 44 seconds as their official record breaking song.

223) June 28

This was meaner than hell!

Were you there for The WWF "King of the Ring" pay-per-view show? It featured the famous "Hell in a Cell" match between Mankind (Mick Foley) and the Undertaker (Mark Callaway). At one moment the Undertaker threw Mankind off the top of the cage. Falling 16 feet he crashed onto the Spanish Announce table. Mankind never recovered and was eventually pinned for the loss. For many wrestling fans, this match was arguably the best "Hell in the Cell" match ever. The video of "the fall" has become one of the most viewed events in WWF history.

Also that night, 17,087 fans saw Ken Shamrock defeat The Rock to win the King of the Ring Tournament while in the main event Kane whipped "Stone Cold" Steve Austin to win the WWF Championship in a "first blood rules" match.

Did you know the tagline for this "King of the Ring" show was "Off With Their Heads"?

224) July 1

Pittsburgh Post-Gazette praises Plant and Page

Former Led Zeppelin duo Jimmy Page and Robert Plant teamed up for another great concert in the Burgh. At one point during the show Page seemed to have a problem with his equipment. Plant observing the situation, quipped to the audience "It seems Jimmy has lost his knob," which sent the crowd into laughter. Even Page got a chuckle out of the situation. Despite this tiny glitch, Page was all business as he ripped through classic songs all night. His guitar prowess still intact, fans got a taste of his genius on songs such as: The Wanton Song, Bring It On Home, Heartbreaker, Ramble On, No Quarter, Going to California, Tangerine, Gallows Pole, Babe I'm Going To Leave You, Whole Lotta Love and many other favorites. Plant, not lacking from any post-Zeppelin blues commanded his voice and stage like a possessed demon. The charismatic front man still had the pipes to deliver the goods.

Did you know in the next days' Pittsburgh Post-Gazette newspaper, critic Ed Masley said the concert "may have been the arena-rock show of the decade?"

225) November 19

Was this a long recess from school or what?

On this day The Civic Arena held its first ever "Reading Rally". Almost 11,000 students and 1,000 adults gathered to celebrate the joy of reading. The kids, all second and third graders enjoyed a morning like no other. After being bused to the Civic Arena the children found their way to their makeshift seats. Once settled, Mark Milovats, singer, performer and Penn-Trafford elementary school teacher ran out to the mat on center ice and shouted out "Reading is Power!" The youngsters cheered boisterously in appreciation. For the next hour city school officials, television personalities (i.e. Mr. McFeely from "Mister Roger's Neighborhood"), students from the Pittsburgh High School for the Creative and Performing Arts and many city area mascots including Pirate Parrot and Purple Panda were cheerleaders for reading. Children enjoyed listening to stories and songs all in the hope of getting them hooked on the written word.

Did you know after the Reading Rally, children received books donated from The Grable Foundation and Heinz Endowments? As for the adults, some donned a pair of skates and took a spin around the ice.

226) November 29

A Titanic presentation from a petite performer

Were you there for Celine Dion's sold-out concert? This was only the second time that the French Canadian pop diva played at the Civic Arena. The theme of the night was love. Dion sang a variety of love songs in a variety show format. She presented cover songs like The First Time Ever I Saw Your Face and All By Myself and even sang If Only Love Could Be Enough in French. A unique part of the show was the stage set-up. It was an in-the-round and featured platforms that moved up and down with her musicians. The floor of the stage was lit with a neon green heart.

Some local elementary school kids got a special treat this night. Twenty-four of them were earlier selected to sing back-up vocals for Dion. They joined the performer in the opening song called Let's Talk About Love.

This concert was originally scheduled September 12, 1998 but was canceled when a lighting rig crashed to the stage that day.

Did you know fellow Quebecer Mario Lemieux was one of the fans at the Dion concert? He took a bow when Celine acknowledged him.

1999

227) January 30

The "House" rules!

This WWE House Show broke a record. The 18,150 who came out were part of the largest attendance ever at any Civic Arena event.

The boisterous wrestling fans who packed the arena saw a plethora of matches. One of the highlights came when WWF World Champion Mankind disposed of three of the biggest names in the business-the Undertaker, the Big Bossman and the Rock.

In one of the stranger hookups that night, WWFIC Champion Ken Shamrock defeated Billy Gunn by disqualification. It seems Gunn wouldn't release the ankle lock once the champion grabbed the ring ropes and then shoved the referees out of the way when they tried to make him break the hold. After the bout Shamrock hit a belly to belly suplex on several referees.

228) March 11

I've been missing you...

The Rolling Stones finally made their way back to the Igloo. This concert marked the first time the veteran band played the Civic Arena since July 22, 1972. At that time they participated in the KQV Summer Festival of Rock and had just released the double album Exile on Main St. which produced the singles Tumbling Dice and Happy.

On this March night with a sold-out crowd of 17,500 and tickets selling upwards to $250.00, the show would become the highest grossing event in the history of the Civic Arena.

The bared down no gimmick-type of concert saw the slender but fit 55 year-old Jagger command the floor like he was 25. It all started as he entered the stage wearing black leather and shades and jumped around like a young buck. He and his bandmates then filled the night with a mix of old and new songs. Some of the classic ones were: Jumpin'Jack Flash, Gimme Shelter, Honky Tonk Woman, Paint It Black, It's Only Rock and Roll, Start Me Up and

Sympathy for the Devil. One of the best parts of the show came when Mick and the boys walked through a long ramp into a middle stage (in the round). Once there they got down with some vintage numbers like: Route 66, When the Whip Comes Down and Midnight Rambler.

229) July 24

The luck of the Irish

The Irish Tenors teamed up with the Royal Philharmonic as they delighted the Civic Arena crowd. Fashioned after the original Three Tenors, the Irish lads were John McDermott, Anthony Kearns and Ronan Tynan. Throughout the evening each tenor sang solo and as a trio. Their repertoire included a variety of classic and contemporary Irish tunes that included: Who Threw the Overalls in Mrs. Murphy's Chowder, Danny Boy, Only Our Rivers Run Free, Voyage, Boulavogue, Grace, When You Were Sweet Sixteen, Spanish Lady and Go Lassie, Go. One of the highlights of the evening came when Tynan sang The Town I Loved So Well-it brought the audience to their feet.

Tynan, who hails from Johnstown (County Kilkenny, Ireland), displayed a good set of pipes. His voice however is not the only thing he has to his credit. Tynan is a doctor of sports medicine and an award winning disabled athlete. McDermott ironically is not Irish! He was born in Scotland but raised in Canada. Kearns, 27 years old at the time, originally studied catering and hotel management before winning a national vocal competition called "Ireland's Search for a Tenor."

Did you know The Royal Philharmonic is Great Britain's national orchestra?

230) October 22

Some women get a kick out of it

On this night the USA Woman's Soccer Team took on the World All-Stars in the first exhibition game as part of the "Toys 'R' Us Indoor Victory Tour (Ball-off-the Wall). If you recall, Team USA won the 1999 FIFA Women's World Cup on July 10th at the Rose Bowl in Pasadena. After their victory an exhibition tour was set up to celebrate and promote soccer to a greater American audience specifically young women and girls.

In Pittsburgh, 9,875 came out to recognize their soccer heroes. For starters each fan received a mini-soccer ball, T-shirt and autographs just for showing up. In addition, some lucky young girls got to practice in a pre-game warm-up with Team USA while at half-time some youths participated in a shoot-out against goal keeper Saskia Webber. The one and only boy from the group scored the lone goal.

In terms of the exhibition game itself the American women came out a little flat and quickly fell behind 3-1. After finding their legs they scored 8 out of the next 9 goals to take a commanding lead. The World-All Stars scored a couple more but it was too little to late as they lost 9-6.The scorers for the USA side were Cindy Parlow with three goals, Mia Hamm, Julie Foudy and Joy Fawcett with 2 each.

The World All-Stars comprised of players from Japan, China, Mexico, Sweden and Canada. They would face Team USA 11 more times as part of the Victory Tour and compiled a 7-5 win/loss record.

Did you know when Team U.S.A. women's team won the gold medal at the 1999 FIFA World Cup they beat China 5 to 4? All goals were scored in the penalty shootout with Brandi Chastain getting the winner. The attendance that day was 90,185-the largest ever to witness a woman's sporting event in history.

231) December 30

Jagr loves New York

Were you there when the Pittsburgh Penguins, before a sell-out crowd of 17,073 pounded the New York Islanders 9-3? Jaromir Jagr put on an offensive display when he scored 3 goals and collected 4 assists for a 7-point night! It was the first time Jagr got that many points in a game. Fans were appreciative of his accomplishments especially a couple in particular-his parents.

Jaromir Jagr would go on to win the 1999-2000 NHL scoring race with a total of 96 points? This would be his fourth NHL scoring title.

Did you know a few weeks before Jagr scored his 7 points, legendary coach Herb Brooks (remember the "Miracle On Ice) took over as the bench boss while a few months prior to this Mario Lemieux bought the Pittsburgh Penguins team?

2000

<u>232) January 22</u>

Wings get clipped in "Crossfire"

The Pittsburgh Crossefire clipped the Philadelphia Wings 16-15 when Kip Fulks scored on a rifle shot with 27 seconds left in the game. Thus ended the first regular season game of the Crossefire in the National Lacrosse League. The Crossefire would be the second professional lacrosse to debut at the Pittsburgh Mellon Arena but like their predecessors the "Pittsburgh Bulls" they would also fold. Unfortunately this was their first and only season.

The announced crowd for the game was 4,521 but looked like a couple thousand stayed home. Despite the low turnout the Crossefire put on a good show and got some good performances from some key players. Neil Doddridge had 6 points while star player Gary Gait had 5. Kip Fulks not only had the winning goal but added 2 more and an assist. He was also named the game's MVP.

<u>233) January 31</u>

Was that WWF woman champion really a woman?

The WWF- Monday Night Raw treated the 'Burgh to a strange night. First, The Rock defeated hometown boy Kurt Angle-who was pinned for the first time ever. Then in a surprise, former WCW and future WWE Superstars Chris Benoit, Eddie Guerrero, Dean Malenko and Perry Saturn (known then as the radicalz) show up as "friends" of Al Snow and Steve Blackman (Head Cheese) and jumped on the New Age Outlaws during a WWF World Tag Team Title defense. On the same evening Harvey Wippleman (born Bruno Lauer) disguised himself as a woman called "Hervina" and defeated "The Kat" in a Lumberjill Snowbunny" match. The match was contested in a swimming pool full of "fake" snow and surrounded by lady wrestlers.

Did you know Harvey Wippleman became the only male to have won the WWF Women's Championship?

234) March 10

Crossefire brothers put on a show but goalie opens with a bang

Were you there when the Rochester Knighthawks defeated the Pittsburgh Crossefire 17-12 in lacrosse action? Crossefire teammates and brothers Paul and Gary Gait combine to score more than half (7) of Pittsburgh's goals. Paul ended the night with 3 goals and 2 assists while Gary had 4 goals and 4 assists. Gary would also become the first player in league history to surpass 600 career points.

Another highlight of the evening came early on for the 5,325 fans. Crossefire goalie Devin Dalep actually scored the first goal of the contest when his long pass, missed by a teammate ended up behind Rochester netminder Pat O'Toole. Despite the early advantage the Crossefire faded in the third quarter as Rochester scored 9 goals. The Knighthawks were led by Tim Soudan with 5 goals and an assist and was named the game's MVP.

Did you know Devin Dalep's goal was only the second one scored by a goalie in pro indoor lacrosse history?

235) March 18

Old friends patch up their differences

Crosby, Stills, Nash and Young (CSNY) found their rhythm this night. For four guys pushing the 60-year mark, they did a masterful job pleasing their Pittsburgh audience. Fans heard a plethora of classic favorites that included: Eight Miles High (from the Byrds), Southern Man, Stand and Be Counted, Almost Cut My Hair, Cinnamon Girl, Teach Your Children, After the Gold Rush (with Young playing the pipe organ and harmonica), Woodstock, Ohio, Down by the River and Rockin' in the Free World.

Pittsburgh Post Gazette weekend editor Scott Mervis must have been impressed also stating, "Young blew through the Mellon Arena like a hurricane Saturday night and you had to grab hold of something to stay standing." For the record 17,000 fans showed up.

Did you know this was the first time in 25 years CSNY actually toured together? They did make an album in the late 1980's and appeared for a song at Live Aid in Philadelphia in July, 1985 but that was the extent of their collaboration.

<u>236) April 1</u>

April Fools on the ice

In an ugly affair the Thomas Jefferson Jaguars crushed Archbishop Carroll Patriots 6-1 in high school hockey action. Though this was the Jaguars third consecutive Class AA championship in the Pennsylvania Cup finals the game was marred by a load of unsportsmanlike conduct. The referees called a total of 162 penalty minutes including 151 in the third period alone! To add insult to injury, after the rough game, a bench-clearing brawl ensued that carried over into the stands. Before the night was over 8 players had been ejected along with several fans.

At a later date and upon review of the melee officials from the Pennsylvania Interscholastic Hockey League and Thomas Jefferson High School agreed that guidance from a statewide athletic association for administrative purposes was needed.

For the record, on that same evening at the Mellon Arena, Serra Catholic beat Pennsbury 4-1 in the "A" finals while Bethel Park (Pittsburgh) captured the "AAA" title with a 3-1 victory over Father Judge (Philadelphia).

Did you know because of the after game brawl in the Class AA championships, the Thomas Jefferson Jaguars received their winning medals and trophies in the dressing room instead of on the ice?

<u>237) May 4-5</u>

Can I go to bed already?

Were you there when the Philadelphia Flyers defeated the Pittsburgh Penguins 2-1in a playoff game that seemed to last forever? The scene was the fourth game of the Eastern Conference Final and the teams were notched up at 1 goal apiece after regulation play. Overtime started and the battle of Pennsylvania continued. Neither the visiting Flyers nor the Pens could muster a goal in sudden death. Then the night grew longer as a second, third and fourth extra period was needed. Penguin fans who endured the endless match got tired and restless but stuck it through. Some, needing to be at work the same morning slowly trickled out. As the fifth overtime started players and fans alike were exhausted. However, the game needed to go on. Ten minutes passed but still no goal. Then at 7:59 Flyers Keith Primeau ended the marathon affair when he deked out Pens defenseman Darius Kasparaitis and fired a wrist shot past Ron Tugnutt. The building turned quiet and cold as the remaining dejected fans filed out. The two teams, exhausted after in this historical battle, had just played an incredible 92 minutes and 1 second of overtime hockey-the third longest in NHL history. Though the game ended at 2:35 am (7 hours after it started) surprisingly about half of the 17,148 fans stayed until the end.

Some statistics from this historical night included: Pittsburgh and Philadelphia combined for 130 shots on goal-second most in NHL history. Speaking about shots, the Penguins scored on their first shot of the game then went 149 minutes and 36 seconds (equivalent to about 2.5 games) without getting another one. The toll on the players was heavy also. For example, before the game Jaromir Jagr weighed 230 pounds. However, after playing 59 minutes and 8 seconds he dropped to 223 lbs.

Did you know this was the longest played NHL game since April 24, 1936?

238) May 6

The boy from the "Rock" tames the "Hammer"

On this night local boxer and undefeated IBF lightweight champion Paul "The Pittsburgh Kid" Spadafora (McKees Rock) beat Mike "the Hammer" Griffith with a controversial decision. The scheduled 12-rounder was called in the 10th round when Dr. Lawrence Biskin noticed a huge cut over Griffith's right eye. Ironically, the cut came as a result of an accidental head butt by Spadafora in the 4th round.

In addition to featuring a hometown boy in the bout this was a special night. First, for fans watching at home, it was the premiere episode of the new HBO boxing series called "KO Nation." Second, the professional boxing match was the first one held at the Mellon Arena since 1990 and third, the 7,500 fans got to witness 6 preliminary matches.

Did you know because of the extended Penguin/Flyer game held on May 4 (see previous moment), the HBO production crew who were televising the fight had to circle the Mellon Arena several hours looking for a parking space? They couldn't start working until 4:00am on May 5 (an hour and half after the sudden death goal) to convert the arena from hockey to boxing.

239) June 23-24

Keeping the faith

The Promise Keepers "Go the Distance" meetings got serious about the Lord. On these days over 13,000 fathers, sons and male friends gathered at the Mellon Arena. They listened to a group of Christian speakers and renewed their commitment to God, family, community and leadership. Attendees, who came as far as Ohio and New Jersey, heard a variety of inspirational stories and testimonials. This was also a milestone gathering for Promise Keepers as it marked the 100th meeting in its history.

Did you know Promise Keepers was started in 1990 by Bill McCartney (then football coach of the University of Colorado) and Dave Wardell Ph.D.? In 1997 it had its largest gathering when an estimated 1 million men converged on the National Mall in Washington, D.C.

240) September 15

Welcome to the league boys!

The Pittsburgh Penguins squeaked by the Columbus Blue Jackets 3-2. This was a unique moment for the Columbus team as it was their first ever NHL game in franchise history. Though the Blue Jackets came out on the losing end, they were nonetheless glad being it was only a pre-season game.

If you were at the game you may recall who played goal for the Penguins in the second half. He was Pittsburgh product Mark Scally (Coraopolis). Scally went to Moon High School and Penn State University where he got a civil environmental engineering degree. He had an excellent game holding the Blue Jackets to just 1 goal in 17 shots.

Did you know the Columbus Blue Jackets made their first playoff appearance in 2009? Unfortunately they got swept in the first round 4 games to 0 by the Stanley Cup finalists Detroit Red Wings.

241) December 27

Super Mario makes a comeback

Were you there when the Pittsburgh Penguins defeated the Toronto Maple Leafs 5-0 on this historical night? Thirty-five year old Mario Lemieux came out of retirement to play his first game in 44 months. The sold-out crowd didn't have to wait long to get excited. Just thirty-three seconds into the contest Lemieux collected an assist on a goal by co-star Jaromir Jagr. Ironically this was the first point scored by an owner of an NHL team. By night's end Mario had cemented his comeback finishing with 3 points (a goal and 2 assists). His partner in crime for many years, Jaromir Jagr, was one better with 2 goals and 2 assists.

The build up to this game was simply incredible. In the Penguins morning practice 60 reporters were on hand to interview Mario. Meanwhile tickets on eBay were selling for $1,000 while closer to face-off time scalpers outside the Igloo were getting $750 a pop. Penguin officials anticipating the buzz opened the Mellon Arena doors a half an hour early so fans could be seated for the pre-game skate. Even the old retractable dome got some attention too as a huge spotlight flashed *Mario 66* on it. Just before the game, Mario's retired number 66 banner, aloft in the rafters, was lowered to the ice surface and neatly put away. While all this was going on, the scoreboard flashed a picture of Mario's son Austin's awestruck face. Four-year old Austin finally got to see his dad play live for the first time. The game was a family affair for Mario as his wife, children, mother Pierrette and father Jean-Guy were in attendance.

Did you know Lemieux played 43 games this season and scored an incredible 35 goals and added 41 assists?

242) December 30

Two great Penguins reach significant milestones

Three nights after Mario Lemieux made his famous comeback his Pittsburgh Penguins defeated the Ottawa Senators 5-3. In the game Jaromir Jagr became only the fourth European-born NHL player to record 1000 points in his career when he scored a goal in the second period. He finished the night with three points. Not to be outdone, Super Mario Lemieux recorded his 1500th career point. He became only the 10th NHL player to accomplish this feat. Lemieux ended the evening with four points including the assist on Jagr's 1000th point. Both Jagr and Lemieux received standing ovations for their accomplishments.

Did you know it took Lemieux only 747 games to reach 1,500 points? Jagr got his 1,000[th] point in 763 games.

1996

204. Pittsburgh Post-Gazette, February 24, 1996 Page Number C-1&C-2

205. Pittsburgh Post-Gazette, March 27&28, 1996 Page Number C-1

206. www.mcdonalds.com/usa/news/2005/conpr_02092005.html

207. http://www.mag7.net/faq/textfaq.html

1997

208. http://letsgopens.com/penshist.htm

208. http://sports.espn.go.com/nhl/news/story?id=2304706

209. Pittsburgh Post-Gazette, March 15, 1997 Page Number A-1&DD-3

210. Pittsburgh Post-Gazette, March 17, 1997 Page Number DD-1&DD-3

211. Pittsburgh Post-Gazette, April 25, 1997 Page Number 35

211. en.wikipedia.org/wiki/Lord_of_the_Dance_(musical)_tour_dates

212. Pittsburgh Post-Gazette, June 14, 1997 Page Number D-14

212. Pittsburgh Post-Gazette, June 17, 1997 Page Number D-1

213. Pittsburgh Post-Gazette, June 22, 1997 Page Number D-5

213. en.wikipedia.org/wiki/1997_NHL_Entry_Draft

214. Pittsburgh Post-Gazette, July 15, 1997 Page Number A-5

215. Pittsburgh Post-Gazette, August 3, 1997 Page Number B-7

216. Pittsburgh Post-Gazette, October 18, 1997 Page Number D-12"

216. Pittsburgh Post-Gazette, October 26, 1997 Page Number W-1

217. www.lcb.state.pa.us/webapp/Legal/PublicAdjudicationDisplay.asp?adjudication_sequence=253&adjudication

218. http://mysite.verizon.net/vze7mp9n/id20.html

218. Pittsburgh Post-Gazette, November 20, 1997 Page Number D-6 & BB

219. Pittsburgh Post-Gazette, December 7, 1997 Page Number G-3

1998

220. Pittsburgh Post-Gazette, March 19, 1998 Page Number B-1

220. http://www.elvis.com/concert/schedule/previous.asp

220. http://www.abfla.com/2000/5events.html

221. Pittsburgh Post-Gazette, March 22, 1998 Page Number D-1

221. sports.espn.go.com/nhl/halloffame07/columns/story?columnist=burnside_scott&id=3107427

222. Pittsburgh Post-Gazette, April 20, 1998 Page Number A-1&15

223. Pittsburgh Post-Gazette, April 22, 1998 Page Number E-6

223. http://thejok.tripod.com/id19.htm

223. en.wikipedia.org/wiki/King_of_the _Ring_(1998)

224. http://www.cnn.com/WORLDBEAT/tourdates/1998/06/05/ppp.html

224. http://www.tightbut loose.co.uk/010798html

225. Pittsburgh Post Gazette, November 20, 1998

226. Pittsburgh Post-Gazette, September 12, 1998 Page Number B-12

226. Pittsburgh Post-Gazette, September 13, 1998 Page Number C-1

226. Pittsburgh Post-Gazette, November 30, Page Number B-2

1999

227. http://www.fortunecity.com/athena/thatcher/2042/Mellon.htm

227. http://www.thestoryofwwe.com/99.htm

228. Pittsburgh Post-Gazette, March 12, 1999 Page Number B-1

228. Pittsburgh Post-Gazette, March 13, 1999 Page Number D-10

229. http://www.encyclopedia.com/doc/1G1-54785645.html

229. Pittsburgh Post Gazette, July 26, 1999

230. http://www.concacaf.com/Signals.asp?id=10/26/1999@year=1999

230. http://en.wikipedia.brg/wiki/1999_FIFA_Women's_World_Cup

231. http://mysite.verizon.net/vze7mp9n/id51.html

231. http://en.wikipedia.org/wiki/Jarom%C3%ADr_J%C3%A1gr

2000

232. http://www.lacrosse-network.com/outsidersguide/game0003phpi.htm

233. www.solie.org/titlehistories/wmnswwf.html

233. www.100megsfree4.com/wiawrestling/pages/other/timelin5.htm

234. Pittsburgh Post-Gazette, March 11, 2000 Page Number D-9

235. Pittsburgh Post-Gazette, March 17, 2000 Page Number 23

235. Pittsburgh Post-Gazette, March 20, 2000 Page Number D-1

236. Pittsburgh Post-Gazette April 2, 2000 Page Number D-11

236. Pittsburgh Post-Gazette April 6, 2000 Page Number S-19

237. www.post-gazette.com/pg/07101/776784-61.stm

238. Pittsburgh Post-Gazette, May 7, 2000 Page Number D-1

239. Pittsburgh Post-Gazette June 25, 2000 Page Number B-1

239. www.promisekeepers.org/about/pkhistory

240. Pittsburgh Post-Gazette, September 16, 2000 Page Number D-2

241. Pittsburgh Post-Gazette, December 28, 2000 Page Number A-1

241. http://www.ctv.ca/Servlet/ArticleNews/Story/CTVNews/20001227/ctvnews81064/CTV NewsAt11?s_name=

242. Pittsburgh Post-Gazette, December 3, 2000 Page Number D-1

Chapter 9, 2001-2005

2001

<u>243) January 5</u>

Penguins honor a rookie that left too soon

The Montreal Canadiens defeated the Pittsburgh Penguins 4-3. In a pre-game ceremony, in front of a standing room crowd, the Penguins retired only their second jersey in team history-that of Michel Briere number 21. Briere had played his rookie season in 1969-70 and managed to score 12 goals and collect 32 assists-third best on the team. In the play-offs that year-the first appearance ever for the Penguins, Briere scored the first overtime goal in franchise history. That goal on April 12, 1970 in Oakland, gave Pittsburgh a 4 games to 0 series sweep of the Seals. In the next series the Penguins lost to St. Louis but Briere's future looked bright and promising. Then in the off season, tragedy struck. On May 5, 1970 Briere was fatally injured in a single car crash with 2 friends. The accident happened in Val d'Or, Quebec just 70 miles from his hometown of Malartic. Briere suffered severe injuries that left him in a coma. On April 13, 1971 almost a year after his accident Briere passed away. He was only 21.

Did you know Michel Briere's jersey number 21 was retired 9 days after Mario Lemieux's jersey number 66 was taken down from retirement?

<u>244</u>) January 6

Sale turns into three ring circus!

On this day memorabilia from the recently destroyed Three Rivers Stadium was sold in auction style at the Mellon Arena. Unfortunately organizers of the event underestimated the size of the crowd (~12,000) resulting in a chaotic day. A big part of the problem came from the lack of spotters available to serve the crowd. For example some bids were either ignored or missed completely. Those lucky enough to have winning bids faced further frustrations. As folks went to pay for their lucky possessions they encountered endless lines. Some people waited hours to claim their piece of Pittsburgh history due to a shortage of cashiers. All who finally made it to the front were slapped with an additional 17% fee (7% Allegheny County Sales Tax plus a 10% auction fee). One lady after being in line for hours endured the worst fate as she was told her winning items were gone.

Added to the chaos on the floor was the question of food and drink. As the 10-hour auction proceeded people naturally got hungry and thirsty. Unfortunately only one concession stand was opened-not nearly enough to serve the masses. Again, frustration was the order of the day.

Later, when the auction was over, Stephen Leeper the boss of Three Rivers Stadium admitted that organizers did a number of "bonehead things". However, at the end of the day financially speaking the event did prove profitable. Over $1.1 million was raised in addition to $500,000 from an earlier online auction.

Some of the items and winning bids at the auction included: 6 stadium seats for $2,100, used bases $1,500, framed photo of Roberto Clemente $1,300, locker room first aid kit $800 and a locker room trash can $175.

Did you know the first items sold that day were a pair of lower-level, blue, floor mounted seats? They went for $875 to a Mr. Bob Jones. By the way, Mr. Jones from Beaver Falls had won $54 million in the Pennsylvania Lottery "Super 6" drawing in November 1998.

<u>245</u>) February 3

Pittsburgh pays homage to Hornets hockey

On this day the Wilkes-Barre Scranton Penguins, the AHL farm team of the Pittsburgh Penguins, played a tribute game against the Cincinnati Mighty Ducks. The Baby Pens honored the last AHL team in Pittsburgh the Hornets by wearing their red-on-white sweaters. The colors matched those of the Detroit Red Wings who were the Hornets parent club at the time. The jerseys also had a hornet (wasp) logo and a Baby Pens patch on the shoulder.

Before the game a banner was raised celebrating the three Hornets' Calder Cup Championships in 1952, 1954 and 1967. On hand for the opening ceremonies were ex-Hornet players Billy Harris, Joe Daley, Ab McDonald and Val Fonteyne.

246) March 24

These women got game!

On this day the Mellon Arena hosted its first ever Women's NCAA Basketball East Regional Semi-Finals. In one game Louisiana Tech (No. 3) defeated Missouri (No. 10) 78-67. Takeisha Lewis led the Tech squad with 27 points and 17 rebounds (both personal career highs). Meanwhile Louisiana star Brooke Lassiter had a hot hand also and collected 25 points, 5 rebounds and 7 assists. Her 2 spectacular baskets late in the game sealed the victory.

In the other game, number 1 ranked and defending national champs Connecticut took on North Carolina State (4). In front of a crowd of 9,021 Connecticut scored the first 12 points of the game and never looked back. They cruised to a 72-58 victory with Diana Taurasi pumping in 24 points. Sue Bird added 16 for the Huskies while Pittsburgh native Swin Cash contributed 11.

247) March 26

The best ladies draw a crowd

In the Finals of the Women's NCAA Basketball East Regional Connecticut (1) crushed Louisiana Tech (3) 67-48. Playing another strong game for the Huskies was freshman Diana Taurasi. She scored 17 points including back-to-back 3 pointers which proved to be turning points in the game. Taurasi also added 10 rebounds, 4 assists and was named East Region's Most Outstanding player. Her Connecticut teammate Tamika Williams had a game high 18 points with 10 rebounds, coming off the bench. McKeesport product Swin Cash finished with 10 and celebrated victory in her home town.

This game broke an attendance record for a women's basketball game in Pittsburgh when 9,397 fans came through the turnstiles!

Did you know Notre Dame were the 2001 Women's National champs? Connecticut would win it in 2002, 2003 and 2004.

248) June 12

Will that guarantee me money in the bank?

Were you there when the "Success 2001" tour across the USA hit the Mellon Arena with some big personalities? Ex-president Bill Clinton got things going with a bang when he was introduced with orchestra music and a blast of red, white and blue confetti. The charismatic Clinton then captured his audience for 20 minutes while talking about the importance of leadership and teamwork. Following the ex-President were other big name motivational gurus that included: Canadian Peter Lowe, co-founder of the "Success-style" seminar tours, author and salesperson Zig Ziglar, politician Elizabeth Dole (spouse to 1996 Republican Presidential nominee Bob Dole), real estate giant Tom Hopkins, legal advisor Robert Bluhm, investor Phil Town, television host of America's Most Wanted John Walsh, ex-Steelers great Terry Bradshaw and Larry King (via satellite). All spoke on themes such as: commitment to change, teamwork and willingness to take a risk.

The "Success 2001" tour attracted 6,000 people from various professional backgrounds. Some were insurance agents, sales personnel, middle managers, real estate moguls and a few Amish furniture vendors with their wives.

Did you know outside the Mellon Arena some people were protesting Clinton's visit?

249) June 17-18

The Steelers were looking for a few hundred good men and women

On these two days the Pittsburgh Steelers converted the Mellon Arena into a huge interview office for their Job Fair. The Black and Gold brass were looking to hire 1000 people for event-day jobs at the newly constructed Heinz Field. All positions were part-time and included: ticket takers, sellers, ushers, security personnel, concession employees and club and suite attendants. Folks wanting to be part of the Steelers family came with resumes in tow. In fact one hundred of them were waiting in line before the doors even opened. Once inside, ap-plicants were steered toward particular interview tables. Some with the right qualifications were hired on the spot.

Did you know the Job Fair was conducted from 11am to 7pm each day?

250) August 31

Let's start the school year off with a bang!

On this day the Pittsburgh Public Schools System held a "special" meeting for its nearly 5,200 employees. The purpose was to jump start the new academic year in a fun way. It started quickly as teachers arrived at the arena. Once gathered, they marched Olympic-style in a "parade of schools" carrying placards with their school names as fellow colleagues cheered them on. Others had flags, pictures of mascots and banners to promote their school. As the procession ended participants were seated and awaited the next interesting moment. Superintendent John Thompson then turned the pep rally themed morning into a party. Music, prizes, motivational speeches and jokes continued to fill the jovial atmosphere. At one point guest speaker Gary Griesser upon finishing his speech joined Superintendent Thompson in singing a rendition of "The Impossible Dream". Once the song was over the audience chuckled at the unlikely duo. Not wanting to leave on that "note" Thompson quickly retorted "I want to thank you all for coming to my birthday party. That's why you're here right?" The crowd then busted out laughing as they stood and applauded profusely.

251) September 23

Some unforgettable moments at the "Unforgiven"

On this day the WWE presented "Unforgiven 2001." This was the first WWE pay-per-view show after the events of 9/11. In honor of the victims, two-time Grammy Award winner Jennifer Holliday started the evening singing "America the Beautiful." At the end of her performance the sold-out crowd gave Holliday a rousing ovation.

As fans settled in, they awaited various matches including the one featuring Pittsburgh native Kurt Angle. Angle, the 1996 Summer Olympic heavyweight freestyle wrestling gold medal winner didn't disappoint. He beat "Stone Cold" Steve Austin when Austin submitted after the Ankle Lock. After the match Angle celebrated his second WWE Championship as his family gathered in the ring with him.

In another highlight match Dwayne "The Rock" Johnson retained his WCW title when he disposed of Booker T. The Rock used the Rock Bottom (a version of the sidewalk slam) then pinned Booker T. for the victory.

Did you know The Rock once attended Freedom High School in Bethlehem, Pennsylvania? While at the school he was on the football, track and field and wrestling teams.

252) December 13

Ladies taste a "Swede" victory

Were you there when the U.S. Women's Olympic Ice Hockey team (and defending Olympic Champs) pasted Team Sweden 9-1in a tune-up exhibition game for the 2002 Winter Olympics? The Americans out shot their Nordic opponents 51 to 4 while cruising to victory. The 4,624 spectators saw Jenny Potter lead the way with 3 goals and an assist.

Did you know in the Olympic Games at Salt Lake City Team U.S. captured the silver medal losing only to Canada in the final game. Sweden managed to get the bronze.

253) December 22

The last of a basketball tradition, almost

This was supposed to have been the last "City Game" played by the Pittsburgh Panthers and the Duquesne Dukes at the Mellon Arena. After all, one school had a basketball court on campus while the other one was building one. Pittsburgh would soon introduce the 12,500 seat Petersen Events Center while Duquesne had the 5,350 seat A.J. Palumbo Center since 1988. Starting in 2002 the plan was to alternate the "City Game" between the 2 sites. For the most part the two schools stuck to the plan except for the 2009 game. Please see chapter 10 for the details

On this night the Pittsburgh Panthers continued their recent dominance of Duquesne by beating them 78-63. Though the attendance was a respectable 7,103 the atmosphere in the cavernous Mellon Arena had long grown stale. The good old days were gone so the new venues were a much needed shot in the arm.

Did you know of the 34 "City Games" played at the Civic /Mellon Arena until this date Pittsburgh won 20 while Duquesne captured 14?

2002

254) March 15

Men cause mayhem at the Mellon

Five years after successfully hosting parts of rounds one and two of the men's NCAA basketball tournament, the Mellon Arena did it again. On this day fans of March Madness witnessed 4 games from teams in the south and west division. In the closest game the Golden Bears from California defeated the University of Pennsylvania Ivy Leaguers 82-75. The biggest blow out came when No. 1 ranked Cincinnati destroyed Boston University 90-52. The Cincinnati win gave Coach Bob Huggins his 500th career victory. In the other 2 games the UCLA Bruins crushed Mississippi 80-58 while the hometown Pittsburgh Panthers disposed of Central Connecticut State 71-54. Pittsburgh's win was their first in NCAA tournament since 1991. Meanwhile the Connecticut loss ended their 19-game winning streak. The Panthers were led by the injured Brandin Knight who finished with 17 points, 9 assists and 5 steals. The talented Knight would go on to be the Big East co-player of the year as he broke a Pittsburgh season record with 237 assists.

Did you know the crowd of 17,015 would be the second largest ever to witness a Pittsburgh Panther game at the Civic/Mellon Arena? They would match this total 2 days later when they hosted California.

255) March 17

A couple St. Paddy's Day delights

In round two of the men's NCAA basketball tournament the sold-out crowd was treated to 2 absolute gems. In one contest, crowd favorite Pittsburgh Panthers took on California. The game proved to be one of the greatest defensive battles in NCAA history. The stingy Panthers thwarted the Golden Bear shooters often as they eked out a 63-50 victory. In fact California managed only 14 points in the first 17 minutes of the second half-its lowest point total of the season. Their fate was sealed when Pittsburgh went on a 16-0 run late in the third and beginning of the fourth. The Panther win gave them a Sweet Sixteen visit for the first time since 1974. Unfortunately Pittsburgh lost to Kent State 78-73 as the Golden Flashes moved on to the Elite Eight.

In the second game UCLA hosted No.1 ranked Cincinnati in a game for the ages. In some circles it was considered the "best basketball game ever played at the Civic/Mellon arena." In the end UCLA outlasted the Bearcats in double overtime. After the game UCLA point guard Cedric Bozeman elated with the victory was quoted as saying" This game should be on ESPN Classic tomorrow."

Cincinnati started the contest well and through the second half had a comfortable 9-point cushion. UCLA stayed focused and chipped away at the lead. With just over a minute to play they completed their rally and were ahead 80-78. The Bearcats Leonard Stokes then scored on a beautiful spinning shot with 35 seconds left that sent the game into overtime. In the first OT frame Bozeman drained one with 39 seconds left to notch the game at 90. Cincinnati's Immanuel McElroy could have been a hero with 3 seconds left but his 3-pointer failed. In the second overtime UCLA converted some early errant plays that put the game out of reach. They continued to press until the buzzer sounded and won the marathon game 105-101. Their victory, a classic one, came in large part to holding Cincy All-American guard Steve Logan to just 18 points.

Did you know Maryland won the 2002 NCAA basketball tournament? They defeated Indiana 64-52 in the final. It was their first championship in school history.

256) April 28

The final farewell-academically speaking!

On this date the University of Pittsburgh held its last commencement ceremony at the Mellon arena. This marked the end of a 33 year tradition that began in 1969. More than 12,000 people including faculty members, graduates, invited guests, family and friends attended the event.

One unusual sighting at this ceremony was that of graduate Luca Covi. The civil engineering graduate had a doll of Bob the Builder on his graduation cap.

Did you know this commencement ceremony was supposed to be held at the Petersen Event Center on the University of Pittsburgh's campus? Unfortunately the newly constructed center which opened on the same weekend was not quite ready to handle such a crowd.

257) Oct 30-Nov 1

This is better than sitting in class all day!

On these days the "Go for it Road Show" caught the attention of many kids. Some 23,000 local children (third to eight graders) from various Pittsburgh schools attended a 90-minute presentation sponsored by HealthSouth. The goal from HealthSouth, one of the largest health care providers in the nation, was to provide healthy lifestyle messages in a fun atmosphere. The program included laser lights timed to music, relay races through obstacle courses and inflatable sports equipment.

Did you know on March 18, 2003 FBI agents executed search warrants at the headquarters of HealthSouth in Birmingham, Alabama? They were investigating a supposed accounting scandal headed by founder and CEO Richard Scrushy.

258) December 6

This "Church" can pack 'em in!

The holiday season got off with a blast when the Mellon arena presented "A Royal Christmas". Veteran performers Christopher Plummer and Julie Andrews co-hosted the exquisite night of international music and dance. The elaborate show boasted 150 performers from London's Royal Philharmonic Concert Orchestra, the Westminster Concert Choir and Bell Choirs, London's Royal Ballet, Winnipeg's Royal Ballet and the Bolshoi and Kiev Ballet. The evening was filled with a variety of new and traditional performances that included the "Nutcracker".

Guest singer for the evening was young Charlotte Church. Church dazzled the festive crowd with her sweet angelic voice. Her repertoire included such diverse songs as Ave Maria and Bridge Over Troubled Waters.

Did you know souvenir programs for this show sold for $20.00 a pop?

259) December 15

King James holds court

Were you there for the Steel City Hoopla event? Three high school basketball games were played at the Mellon Arena in one day. In the featured event, 17-year old phenomenon Lebron James and teammates from St.Vincent-St.Mary in Akron, Ohio took on New Castle, Pennsylvania. James a senior had garnished national attention for his many exploits. Naturally there was a buzz in the air as folks in Pittsburgh wanted to see the next NBA star. At tip-off St.Vincent-St.Mary and New Castle played hard. Both exchange baskets fairly evenly in the first half. In the second part, the much bigger and talented St.Vincent-St.Mary team took over. The 6'8"James demonstrated his prowess with precision shooting, slam dunks and great defense. Often his plays brought the crowd to their feet. There was no doubt about his talent and skills. As the game wore on New Castle fell further and further behind. As the final buzzer sounded St. Vincent-St. Mary won in convincing fashion 82-48. James finished the game with 32 points (including 5 slam dunks), 14 rebounds, 3 blocks, 3 assists and the adoration of many.

In the preliminary game Chartiers Valley defeated Aliquippa 69-66 while in the final game Sto-Rox edged Hempfield 50 to 49. The attendance that day was 6,624.

Did you know many players from the Steelers were in attendance? Even though Pittsburgh had just completed an afternoon football game at Heinz Field they rushed to the arena to see Mr. James in action.

260) December 22

Rudy gets raunchy!

The "Champions On Ice Tour-25th Anniversary" was something special in more ways than one. Fans attending the event saw brilliant performances from some of the best skaters in the world. Countries like Russia, Canada, France and the United States were represented by stars such as: Victor Petrenko and his triple axels, Elvis Stojko and his quadruple toe loops, Surya Bonaly with her famous back flips, and Nicole Bobek with her signature high leg spirals. However most of the crowd was shocked and awed when American skater Rudy Galindo performed a number wearing a black bustier top, black satin or leather pants, elbow length lacy gloves, silver buckle belt, necklace, glitter and makeup. While skating to the song "Sweet Travestite"/"TimeWarp", he then ripped his pants off. Underneath were a short bottom and fishnet stockings. What a sight for the bewildered crowd!

261) December 29

Oldies but Goodies

On this night the Pittsburgh Doo Wop Holiday Reunion Show got folks thinking of songs from a more innocent time. The show, a trip down memory lane for those who grew up in the 1950's and early 1960's, was the first Doo Wop reunion show ever at the Mellon Arena. Some of the highlight performers included: The Crystals (Da Doo Ron Ron), Johnny Maestro and The Brooklyn Bridge ("Sixteen Candles"), Charlie Thomas's Drifters ("Under the Boardwalk"), Cleveland Still and the Dubs ("Could This Be Magic"), Johnnie and Joe ("Over the Mountain, Across the Sea") and Lou Christie ("Lightning Strikes"). Ironically, one of the bands performing this night at the Mellon Arena was called The Penguins. They performed their hit "Earth Angel".

2003

262) February 26 - March 2

This magic went a little too far!

Were you there for "Disney On Ice-100 Years of Magic?" Performers from 11 different countries skated as characters in such Disney movie classics as: "Toy Story", "Beauty and the Beast", "Aladdin", "Mulan", "A Bug's Life" and "The Lion King". Though audiences enjoyed the shows on the ice, the Disney Company was not so pleased with a particular off-ice event. Apparently after the 7pm show on February 27th, someone performed some magic with the revenues and stole $110,000. The cash came from the sale of stuffed animals, light swords, T-shirts and other Disney merchandise. The Pittsburgh police were later called to investigate. The Disney Company informed them that only 2 people had the key to the money. One of them, the bookkeeper from Field Entertainment never reported to work.

263) March 7

These guys can both tickle the ivory!

On this night Elton John and Billy Joel rocked the Mellon together. The two piano players once again teamed up as part of their successful Face to Face Tour. Started in 1994, the Face to Face Tour proved to be a good formula for the performers while fans got two for the price of one. Tickets prices went for $100.00 a pop but that didn't seem to dampen the enthusiasm of the crowd.

John and Joel played for more than three hours and churned out hit after hit. The show, with a set format, began feverously when both played on twin pianos performing duets. The piano duels included: "Bennie and the Jets" and the Beatles "A Hard Day's Night. With the crowd well pumped up, the concert shifted gears when each performer did a solo set. Elton pounded out 12 fan favorites like "Someone Saved My Life Tonight", "Tiny Dancer", "Take Me to the Pilot" and "Rocket Man." while Joel followed with "Scenes from an Italian Restaurant", "Movin' Out", Innocent Man", "New York State of Mind", "Angry Young Man", and "It's Still Rock 'n' Roll to Me." Both high energy sets had the crowd begging for more. The concert ended when John and Joel paired up again for an encore.

Did you know the 2003 Face to Face Tour by Elton John and Billy Joel made $46 million for just 24 concerts?

264) June 14

Birds of a feather flock together but some "Chicks" ruffle them

On this night the Dixie Chicks brought their "country" music to the Steel City. The concert was interesting for a couple of reasons. One, the set-up was a stage-in-the round that included catwalks leading out to the audience. It also featured a video show with 1.5 million LED lights and during the performance, artificial flowers, grass, trees and even a windmill sprung up from underneath the stage. Secondly, singer Natalie Maines of the "Chicks" said "I don't know if anyone here heard about the ordeal we got into about three months ago?" Of course she was referring to the comment she made about President Bush on March 10, 2003 while performing a concert in London. At the time Maines was quoted "Just so you know, we're ashamed the President of the United States is from Texas." The statement caused a big backlash in the U.S. and for many months radio stations across the country refused to play Dixie Chick songs. Meanwhile back at the Pittsburgh concert some audience members booed Natalie but shortly after, cheers drowned them out. By the way the show was sold out.

Did you know before the Dixie Chicks concert on July 6, 2003 in Dallas, Texas Natalie Maines received a death threat?

265) July 15

Americans love their idols

On this night the Mellon arena welcomed "American Idol Live." The television show that took America by storm also toured the country with its top finalists. After its second season American Idol finally made a stop in Pittsburgh. Over 10,000 fans came out to see winner Ruben "the velvet teddy bear" Studdard, runner-up Clay Aiken, Kimberley Locke, Josh Gracin and company perform songs individually and as a group. The crowd, many of them young girls screamed loudest for Clay Aiken. At one point Aiken retrieved a piece of flying lingerie and yelled "Rueben, I got panties!"

Did you know Rolling Stone magazine once called American Idol the "karaoke death squad?"

<u>266) October 11</u>

The Eagle has finally landed again

The Eagles returned for a long awaited concert. As part of the Eagles Farewell 1 tour the band delighted fans with many of their old favorites. This was the first time "the boys of Summer" played at the Mellon arena since 1979 which coincidently was the last time the band released an album of new material (The Long Run). The Pittsburgh concert showed the strength and diversity of its members with impeccable music and vocals. Glenn Frey was great with "Peaceful, Easy Feeling", "Already Gone" and "Lyin' Eyes" while Don Henley still had the pipes in Hotel California and Sunset Grill. Not taking a back seat to anyone Joe Walsh energized the crowd with "Turn to Stone", Life's Been Good", and "Rocky Mountain Way." Timothy Schmit was even smooth on "I Can't Tell You Why."

At one point in the concert, eccentric Joe Walsh said, "I was going to run for governor of California but decided not to at the last minute because we had a concert in Pittsburgh. The good news is, from now on I'm going to do all the "Terminator" movies."

Did you know in 2003, the Eagles released "Eagles-The Very Best Of?"

<u>267) December 23</u>

A TRANS-sending experience!

Were you there when the Trans-Siberian Orchestra presented "Christmas Eve and Other Stories?" The concert was a monster feast for the ears and eyes. The production was so elaborate it included: an arena-size light, fog and pyro show as well as fake snow and a killer sound system. Combined with the rock-like sounds of the orchestra fans were literally carried on a sensory and emotional journey that gave a whole new meaning to the spirit of Christmas. Some of the moving instrumental favorites were: A Mad Russian's Christmas, Boughs of Holly, Christmas Eve/Sarajevo12/24, Led Zeppelin's Kasmir and a tribute to Emerson, Lake and Palmer's version of Tchaikovsky's Nutcracker Suite.

Did you know the Trans-Siberian phenomenon was started by Paul O'Neill (composer, lyricist and producer) and keyboardist Jon Olivia in 1996? Both were former members of the progressive-metal group Savatage. The Trans-Siberian Orchestra is now a platinum seller juggernaut.

2004

268) February 22

Penguins can't beat anyone

Before 11,780 disappointed spectators the Ottawa Senators doubled up the Pittsburgh Penguins 6-3. With the defeat, the Penguins set the dubious NHL record of 18 consecutive losses (17 in regulation and 1 in overtime). Unfortunately for fans of the team, 14 of those losses came at home. Even worse, the Penguins didn't win a home game in January nor February of the 2003-04 season.

The game was a good one for Ottawa forward Martin Havlat who scored 3 goals including the last one into an empty net.

Did you know before the game Peter Hewlett sang a botched up version of "O, Canada?"

269) April 16-17

This ain't no horse play!

Equestrian lovers made there way to the Mellon arena for the 34th Anniversary Tour of the Lipizzaner Stallions. The famous European horses put on a dazzling display of artistic maneuvers that included the: courbette, levade and mezair. The moves demonstrated the strength and beauty of these majestic beasts.

The dozen white stallions in the show came from a rare and unique breed called Lipizzan. Historically they were trained for military purposes. One demonstration of this background was the capriole-a move in which a horse leaps in mid-air and kicks out with its back hooves, as if striking foot soldiers in battle. This and other battlefield moves were presented in the section "Airs Above the Ground".

At the conclusion of the show the Lipizanner Stallions performed the Grand Quadrille. This featured intricate, equine ballet with moves through the highest level of dressage. The horses pranced, marched and intricately weaved their way across the floor to the music of the Masters.

Did you know many of the Lipizanner Stallions in the tour were born and trained at the Spanish Riding School or Piber Stud Farm both in Austria?

270) June 16

The sounds of silence are finally broken

Were you there for the Simon and Garfunkel concert? After a successful reunion tour in 2003 the boys from Queens, New York did another one in 2004. This time they made it to the Mellon Arena for the first time since 1965. At that time, Paul and Art just 23 years old were the opening act for the Rolling Stones.

On this particular night (almost forty years later) they played all their hits. Fans familiar with the lyrics, and a lot of them were, sung along in unison. The folk-rock duo performed such timeless classics as: Homeward Bound, I Am a Rock, At the Zoo, Baby Driver, Hey, Schoolgirl, Scarborough Fair, Sound of Silence, Mrs. Robinson, Cecilia, Bridge Over Troubled Waters, and The 59th Street Bridge Song (Feelin' Groovy).

Between music sets fans got a special treat. The Everly Brothers, boyhood idols of Simon and Garfunkel teamed up with the pair to sing Wake Up Little Susie, All I Have to Do is Dream and Bye Bye Love.

271) September 30

These people really know how to Hamm it up

The Rock and Roll Gymnastics Championships Tour did a number at the Mellon Arena. Some of the biggest stars from the recently completed 2004 Summer Olympics in Athens, Greece got to perform their stuff again but this time in a friendly competition. Twin brothers Paul and Morgan Hamm, Blaine Wilson, Tasha Schwikert, Svetlana Khorkina and others dazzled audiences with gymnastic routines choreographed to lively music. Hip-hop artist Jojo hosted the show.

Paul Hamm was the all-around gold medalist gymnast at the 2004 Olympics. However if you recall there was a lot of controversy surrounding his win. Some of the judges apparently punched in the wrong scores for a South Korean athlete who may have won the competition. The athlete Yang Tae Young protested the results and later took legal action. A hearing on September 27, 2004 in Switzerland (just three days before this friendly competition) regarding this mix-up lasted 11.5 hours. It adjourned with no conclusion and as a result Paul Hamm retained his gold medal.

272) October 1-10

Hey man these tours are RAD!

On these days the Mello Arena gave free "Behind the Scenes" tours of the building. This was part of "10 **RAD**ical Days" sponsored by the Allegheny **R**egional **A**sset **D**istrict (RAD). At this time RAD also gave free admission and organized special events to many of the fun places in which people in Pittsburgh enjoyed. They included: Carnegie Science Center, the National Aviary, the Pittsburgh Zoo, Heinz Field, PNC Park and of course the Mellon Arena.etc). I guess residents of Allegheny County got to see what their 1% extra sales tax dollars supported.

Did you know the Allegheny Regional Asset District gave the Mellon Arena $3.2 million for debt service in 2004?

273) October 21-24

Blades of danger

On these four days the Mellon Arena got to host the prestigious Skate America competition. Over 60 figure skaters from 16 countries took part in the event. A different aspect of the competition was the new International Skating Union (ISU) judging system. Points were awarded for technical score combined with 5 additional components. They included: skating skills, transitions, performance/execution, choreography/composition and interpretation. Medals were awarded in the usual four categories of women's singles, men's singles, ice dancing and pairs. The winners were. Women's singles = gold, Angela Nikodinov (U.S.), silver, Cynthia Phaneuf (Canada), bronze, Miki Ando (Japan). Men's singles = gold, Brian Joubert (France), silver, Ryan Jahnke (U.S.), bronze, Michael Weiss (U.S.). Ice dancing = gold, Tanith Belbin/Benjamin Agosto (U.S.), silver Galit Chait/Sergei Sakhnovski (Isreal), bronze, Megan Wing/Aaron Lowe (Canada). Pairs = gold, Zhang Dan/Zhang Hao (China), silver, Julia Obertas/Sergei Slavnov (Russia) bronze, Rena Inoue/John Baldwin Jr. (U.S.).

During the pairs competition one of the scariest moments in Civic/Mellon Arena history occurred. Just over 2 minutes into a routine 22-year old Russian skater Tatiana Totmianina violently crashed to the ice when her partner Maxim Marinin slipped while trying a lasso lift. Tatiana's head hit the surface so hard it sent a shock wave throughout the building. The crowd, not knowing what had just happened, stared in disbelief. Motionless for 15 seconds, but what seemed to be an eternity, Tatiana soon received medical attention. Later Totmianina was sent to the Mercy Hospital where she was treated for a concussion and bruising. Fortunately the next day she was released and over time recovered from her injuries.

Did you know 3 medal ceremonies scheduled after the pairs event was cancelled and fans were asked to leave the building?

274) October 28

James soars past Hawks

Were you there when the Cleveland Cavaliers defeated the Atlanta Hawks 99-94 in a much anticipated pre-season game? Cavs' second year star Lebron James scored 16 points while making his return to the Mellon Arena as a professional. The pro-Cleveland crowd of 9,721 cheered "King James" every time he touched the ball. The star athlete didn't disappoint making slam dunks and no look passes all night. In the third period he and teammate Zydrumas Ilgauskas rallied Cleveland from a 12-point deficit as they cruised to victory. Fans of the phenomenon last saw James in Pittsburgh at the Steel City Hoopla Event as a 17-year old whiz kid in December 2002.

Did you know former Pittsburgh Panther star Billy Knight was Atlanta Hawks' general manager?

2005

275) February 20

This is a bloody mess!

The Mellon Arena presented WWE's pay-per-view event "No Way Out-2005" and it got ugly. Some 9,500 ravenous wrestling fans saw John "Bradshaw" Layfield (JBL) retain his WWE gold belt over Big Show in the first ever WWE Barbed Wire Steel Cage Match. During the bloody encounter JBL threw Big Show into the steel cage head-first cutting him open. Another highlight came when JBL escaped the cage by crawling out from under the ring after being chokeslammed through the mat off the top rope by the Big Show.

In other ring action, John Cena defeated hometown boy Kurt Angle in the WWE Championship #1Contender tournament finals. Even the referee got roughed up in this one when he was unceremoniously knocked down at one point. Cena's victory earned him a championship match at WrestleMania 21.

Chavo Guerrero had an interesting night when he won a 6 Man Elimination Match for the WWE Cruiserweight Championship. The match started with 2 wrestlers and as an elimination occurred the next wrestler entered the ring. Guerrero was the last man standing and thus declared the winner. Finally, fans of The Undertaker were happy when they saw him pin Luther Reigns with a Tombstone piledriver.

Did you know during this "No Way Out" event Joy Giovanni won the 2005 Rookie Diva of the Year competition? Events in the competition included evening gown, talent contest and swimsuit competition. Giovanni received 65% of the on-line votes while beating out 3 other women.

276) June 12

These seniors got game!

The 2005 Summer National Senior Games were held in Pittsburgh June 3-18. One of the highlights of this competition was the Celebration of Athletes Event on June 12 at the Mellon Arena. Here over 10,000 athletes aged 50 or older marched Olympic-style through the arena wearing their state uniforms. Each state also had a flag bearer who led participants in the Parade of States. The mayor of Pittsburgh, Tom Murphy and other county and state officials greeted all competitors. Meanwhile former gold medal figure skater Peggy Fleming made a special appearance. Pittsburgh musical groups like Felix Cavaliere (of the Rascals), Lou Christie, The Crystals, Jimmy Beaumont and the Skyliners, The Vogues, The Marcels, The Jaggerz and Johnny Angel and the Halos provided entertainment.

Athletes at the 10th Summer National Senior Games competed in 18 different sports in venues across Pittsburgh. A couple highlights included: Richard Cochran (66 years old) winning the gold medal in the discus event with a toss of 158 feet and 11 inches. Cochran was a former competitor in the 1960 Summer Olympic Games in Rome. Samuel Pate at 103 years old bowled 3 games for an average of 129 and won the gold medal in his category of 100+. Fortunately for Pate he was the only competitor in his age bracket!

On a sadder note Paul V. Haase Jr., 77, of Waverly, Tennessee died of a broken neck while warming up for a cycling event. It had been his third National Summer Senior Games.

Did you know one of the events of the Summer National Senior Games was the triathlon? It consisted of 400 meters of swimming, 20 kilometers of biking and 5 kilometers of running.

<u>277) July 29-31</u>

There's something fishy going on here

On these three days the Mellon Arena was the site of the 35th edition of the CITGO B.A.A.S. (Bass Anglers Sportsmen Society) Master Classic Weigh-Ins. It all started when forty-seven of the nation's best anglers were lured to Pittsburgh for the prestigious fishing competition. All were vying for a share of the $700,000 in prize money. Competitors spent 3 days on the Allegheny, Monongahela and the Ohio rivers trying to reel in the biggest bass within a 100-mile range.

At the final weigh-ins at the Mellon Arena, Michigan's Kevin Van Dam won the tournament in front of a raucous crowd of 13,500. His weight of 12 pounds, 15 ounces beat out Aaron Martens of Alabama by a mere 6 ounces. Van Dam claimed the winning prize of $200,000. Not only was the competition close but a dubious record was set for the lowest weight in the history of the event. By the way, all fish caught for this competition were released back into the rivers.

Did you know ESPN and ESPN2 dedicated 12 hours of television time to the CITGO BASS Master Classic and the city of Pittsburgh received much praise as host of the tournament?

<u>278) August 23</u>

Some famous people get down to business

The "Get Motivated Business Seminar" caused a stir in Pittsburgh in more ways than one. First, it started early when normal city employees were frustrated by the high volume of cars coming into town that day. Added to their morning traffic woes were the 15,000 extra people heading to the business seminar. Secondly, city parking garages quickly filled up causing more frustration for people already late for work. Many were angered on a day that was supposed to bring happiness and motivation.

Once attendees made it to the Mellon Arena, albeit a little frazzled, they quickly got re-stirred in a positive way. The first guest speaker, former New York City mayor Rudolph Giuliani was introduced with a flare. Confetti and streamers were released while Frank Sinatra's, New York, New York was blasted through the air. Giuliani then grabbed the microphone and asked the curious audience whether leaders were born or made? He told them they were made and followed with "Everything is about what you learn, study and emphasize." The former mayor then continued with an informative and engaging speech that set the tone for the day. Others like television's financial guru Suze Orman, America's number one motivator, Zig Ziglar, editor and publisher of Forbes magazine Steve Forbes, businessman Rick Belluzzo and Steelers quarterback Ben Roethlisberger followed with enthusiastic talks.

279) September 22

Pittsburgh bands together for worthy cause

On this night over 8,000 people attended the P.L.E.A.S.E. (Pittsburgh Lends Emergency and Savings Effort) benefit concert for the victims of Hurricane Katrina. The idea for the benefit started when Pittsburgh civic, business, and media organizations, as well as musicians and individuals banded together for the cause of New Orleans. The resulting benefit show held at the Mellon Arena was a virtual Whose Who of local performers. They included: The Clarks, Rusted Root, Donnie Iris, Poverty Neck Hillbillies, Joe Grushecky, Bill Deasy, Good Brother Earl, B.E. Taylor, Crave and Margot B. Non-musical guests that night were: Ex-Steelers Franco Harris and Louis Lipps and KDKA's Larry Rickert (radio) as emcee.

One of the highlights of the concert came when all the artists played the last 2 songs as a group. Together they sang Marvin Gaye's "What's Goin' On" and Buffalo Springfield's "for What It's Worth."

Did you know the P.L.E.A.S.E. benefit concert raised about $100,000?

280) October 8

"The Kid" makes his debut

Were you there when Sid "The Kid" Crosby made his Mellon Arena debut? The capacity crowd of 17,132 had waited all summer to see the NHL's No.1 draft choice skate for them. Sid didn't disappoint when he collected 2 assists and scored his first professional goal. The goal, scored late in the second period against the Boston Bruins brought the crowd to their feet for a standing ovation. The Penguins had a comfortable 6-4 lead at this point and seemed to be heading for their first win. During the next stoppage in play fans started to chant "Croz-bee, Croz-bee." In the third period however Boston scored twice to make it 6-6. The game went to overtime and again the Bruins scored to prevail 7-6. Fans left the building sad knowing the "Beantown" boys had spoiled "The Kid's" coming out party.

If you were at the Mellon Arena that night you may remember Mario Lemieux scoring 2 goals. Lemieux the Penguin captain had turned 40 years old three days before.

Did you know NHL commissioner Gary Bettman was among the spectators that night?

281) October 22

This concert was a "Bono-fide" winner!

U2 put on a great concert this evening as fans got a little taste of everything. It started early as confetti, lights and cheers filled the air with anticipation. Bono then emerged from the middle of the arena with his arms raised as he blew kisses to the crowd. The band ripped into "City of Blinding Lights" and the stage was set for a frenetic evening. Speaking about stages, U2 had a circular platform that extended through the entire section of the arena. In addition a monster lighting set and overhead movie screens gave Bono opportunities to display political and cultural messages. The band played a tight set while churning out a variety of songs from oldies like "Sunday Bloody Sunday" to newer ones like "Elevation".

One lucky die-hard fan had his dream come true when he was plucked from the audience to play acoustic guitar with Edge on "Party Girl". During their performance, Bono sprayed the fans with champagne. Afterwards the crowd gave them both a rousing ovation.

Did you know U2 was inducted into the Rock and Roll Hall of Fame on March 14, 2005? Bruce Springsteen was their presenter.

282) October 30

Basketball returns with a bang, no I mean "Xplosion"

This night saw the return of professional basketball to the city of Pittsburgh. After almost a 35-year absence, the Pittsburgh Xplosion made their Mellon Arena debut as members of the American Basketball Association (ABA). Their opponents, the Indiana Alley Cats, also new to the league were coached by Greg Graham. Graham played under the famous Bobby Knight at Indiana University before going to the NBA for 5 years. The Xplosion were guided by Tom Thacker who performed in both the NBA and ABA in the 1960's. Assisting Thacker was Pittsburgh native and former NBA star Armen "The Hammer" Gilliam. Gilliam acted as the Xplosion's player/coach.

The Xplosion home opener was an exciting one for the fans as it produced 225 points. However the Xplosion fell a little short losing to the Alley Cats 116-109. Some bright spots for Pittsburgh were: DeVaughn Halsel (Point Park University) with 20 points, JaMar Wesley (Fairmont State) with 19 and 41-year old Armen Gilliam with 12 points and 2 blocks.

Did you know Armen Gilliam was selected 2nd overall in the 1987 NBA draft by the Phoenix Suns?

283) November 19

Hometown boys make a little history

On this sold-out night, state rivals the Philadelphia Flyers doubled the score on the Pittsburgh Penguins 6-3. The game was significant locally because it marked the first time ever two native Pittsburgh hockey players (in the NHL) met on Civic/Mellon Arena ice. Ryan Malone (Upper St. Clair) played for the Penguins while R.J. Umberger (Plum) skated for the Flyers. Neither player scored a goal but Umberger ended the night with 1 assist.

Before the 2008-09 NHL season Ryan Malone signed a multi-year contract with the Tampa Bay Lightning while R.J. Umberger was traded to the Columbus Blue Jackets.

Did you know after the Flyers beat the Penguins this night Pittsburgh rookie Sidney Crosby met 2004 National League (baseball) rookie of the year and native Canadian Jason Bay? Bay was in town after signing an $18.25 million contract the week before.

284) November 30

Maybe I need a new set of "Wheels"

On this long night of basketball the Detroit Wheels defeated the Pittsbugh Xplosion 107-93. At 6:56pm the public announcer told the crowd there would be a 10-minute delay. Instead of starting at 7pm it would start at 7:10pm. Well that must have been the longest 10 minutes in history because the game didn't get underway until 8:03pm! The problem as it turned out was a transportation situation with the Detroit bus. I guess the Wheels had a wheel problem.

Did you know at tip-off time there were only 78 fans left in the Mellon Arena?

285) December 16

The best (Le mieux) Penguin hangs up the skates for good

On this night 40-year old Mario Lemieux played his final professional hockey game as a Pittsburgh Penguin. Mario collected one assist as his team lost to the Buffalo Sabres 4-3 (OT). Ironically, on the same day Michel Therrien made his Penguins coaching debut and named 18-year old Sidney Crosby as an alternate captain.

Superstar Mario Lemieux was forced to retire for good this time due to a heart problem called atrial fibrillation-a condition that causes rapid heartbeat. A news conference held at the Mellon Arena on January 24, 2006 made his retirement official. Lemieux's announcement was so significant that news stations in Canada interrupted their coverage of the national election to broadcast it.

Did you know Mario Lemieux finished his career with 690 goals and 1033 assists for 1,723 points in just 915 games? His average of 1.88 points per game was the second best in NHL history. Only Wayne Gretzky had a better one at 1.92.

2001

243. http://www.pittsburghhockey.net/PensPages/66-69ERA/Briere01.html

243. Michel Briere en.wikipedia.org

244. Pittsburgh Post-Gazette, January 9, 2001 Page Number A-1

245. http://www.pittsburghhockey.net/HornetsPages/HornetsTIME1.html

246. Pittsburgh Post Gazette, March 25, 2001

247. Pittsburgh Post-Gazette, March 27, 2001 Page Number A-1

248. Pittsburgh Post-Gazette, June 13, 2001 Page Number A-1

249. Pittsburgh Post-Gazette, June 18, 2001 Page Number C-5

250. Pittsburgh Post Gazette, September 1, 2001

251. Pittsburgh Post-Gazette, September 24, 2001 Page Number D-2

251. http://en.wikipedia.org/wiki/WWE_Unforgiven

252. Pittsburgh Post-Gazette, December 14, 2001 Page Number B-10

253. Pittsburgh Post-Gazette, December 23, 2001 Page Number D-1

2002

254. Pittsburgh Post-Gazette, March 16, 2002 Page Number DD-1 & DD-6

255. Pittsburgh Post-Gazette, March 18, 2002 Page Number C-1

256. http://www.chronicle.pitt.edu/media/pccc020513/lookcommence2002.html

257. Pittsburgh Post-Gazette, October 29, 2002 Page Number G-3

258. Pittsburgh Post-Gazette, December 7, 2002 Page Number C-8

259. http://www.post-gazette.com/highschoolsports/20021216lebron1216p2asp

260. Pittsburgh Post Gazette, December 23, 2003

260. http://rudy-galindo.com/coi8.htm

261. http://www.pittsburghlive.com/x/pittsburghtrib/s_109391.html

2003

262. http://www.pittsburghlive.com/x/pittsburghtrib/s_119591.html

262. Pittsburgh Post-Gazette, March 1, 2003 Page Number D-5

263. Pittsburgh Post-Gazette, March 14, 2003, Page Number 48

264. http://chickoholic.tripod.com/DixieChicks/id2.html

264. http://wikipedia.org/wiki/Top_of_the_World

265. Pittsburgh Post-Gazette, July 17, 2003, Page Number D-3

266. http://www.eaglesfans.com/tour_2003/pittsreviews.htm

266. http://www.smoothjazznow.com/artist_eagles.htm

267. http://www.trans-siberian.com/ontour/tour-archives2001.shtml

2004

268. http://sports.espn.go.com/nhl/recap?gameId=240222016

269. http://www.pittsburghlive.com/x/pittsburghtrib/s_189339.html

269. www.lipizanner.com

270. http://www.thedreamerofmusic.com/tour2004/tour.htm

271. Pittsburgh Post-Gazette, September 28, 2004, Page Number C-3

271. Pittsburgh Post-Gazette, October 1, 2004, Page Number B-9

272. www.carnegielibrary.org/about/pressroom/2004/RADpressrelease092104.pdf

272. Pittsburgh Post-Gazette, October 1, 2004, Page Number W-3

273. http://www.post-gazette.com/pg/04299/401324-139stm

273. Pittsburgh Post Gazette, October 25, 2004

274. http://sports.espn.go.com/nba/recap?gameId=241028005

2005

275. http://en.wikipedia.org/wiki/No_Way_Out_(2005)

276. Pittsburgh Post-Gazette, June 13, 2005 page number A-1

276. http://www.nmseniorolympics.org/newsletter/05fall/newsoct05-1.pdf

277. sports.espncom/outdoors/tournament/classic/news/story?page=tour_05Classic_day3

277. Pittsburgh Post Gazette, July 29-31, August 1, 2005

278. Pittsburgh Post Gazette, August 24, 2005

279. legistar.city.pittsburgh.pa.us/attachments/3183.doc

280. Pittsburgh Post-Gazette, October 9, 2005 page number C-1

281. www.U2gigs.com/show1330.html

282. Pittsburgh Post-Gazette, October 31, 2005 Page Number E-7

283. http://www.pittsburghhockey.net/Common/PghBorn.html

283. http://www.nhl.com/ice/recap.htm?id=2005020301

283. Pittsburgh Post Gazette, November 20, 2005

284. Pittsburgh Post-Gazette, December 1, 2005 page number D-3

285. en.wikipedia.org/wiki/List_of_National_Hockey_League_statistics_leaders

285. http://www.pittsburghlive.com/x/pittsburghtrib/sports/penguins/s_416770.htm

Chapter 10, 2006-2010

2006

<u>286) March 19</u>

Where were you when the lights went out?

Were you there when the Toronto Maple Leafs defeated the Pittsburgh Penguins 1-0 in a "dark game"? It started in the second period when the power at the Mellon Arena went out not once but twice! The first outage lasted 18 minutes. During the delay, designs of a new hockey facility were shown on the Jumbotron scoreboard. Fans seeing this chanted in unison "New A-Re-Na, New A-Re-Na!" Meantime players from both teams skated around the ice to stay loose. When play finally resumed a second blackout hit soon after. This time the referees had enough and sent all players to their respective dressing rooms. At this point, many of the announced crowd of 15,174 made a beeline for the exits. When the third period finally started an extra 7 minutes and 8 seconds were added to the time clock.

As the situation at the Mellon Arena seemed a bit strange, the hockey game itself proved no different. The lone goal of the evening was scored by the Maple Leafs Chad Kilger on a penalty shot! This was the first time in 70 years that an NHL game ended 1-0 via a penalty shot.

As to what caused the blackouts at the Igloo that night, officials of the Penguins said the initial one was a failure of a power line running into the arena. The second outage resulted when Duquesne Light turned on a secondary power system that overrode the primary. When this happened it caused a fire in an electrical panel some 30 yards behind one of the seating sections.

Did you know at the time of the fire no announcement through the public address system was made?

287) April 17

Take a bow Sid!

On this night a Penguin rookie made history as Pittsburgh thumped the New York Islanders 6-1. Sidney Crosby collected 3 assists in the game and in the process became the youngest player in the NHL ever to score 100 points. In appreciation of his feat, 17,084 fans applauded Crosby and showered the ice surface with hats and t-shirts. Ironically the hats and t-shirts were given to spectators before the game as support for the Penguins' efforts to get a new arena. The game was delayed 5 minutes as the Mellon Arena crew gathered up the thrown objects.

This was certainly Crosby's lucky night in more ways than one. Long before the record-breaking applause Sid had received another one. In a pre-game ceremony (the last home game of the season) the crowd showed their support when "The Kid" was honored as the Penguins' MVP of the season. Crosby would eventually finish his rookie year with 102 points and break the Penguins rookie record of 100 held by Mario Lemieux.

Did you know Dale Hawerchuck of the Winnipeg Jets (in1981-82) held the previous distinction of being the youngest player in the NHL to score 100 points? He was 18 years, 354 days old. Crosby did it in 18 years and 253 days.

288) June 29-July1

C'est incroyable!

On these days Cirque Du Soleil's "Delirium" had people begging for more. Fans of the unique arena spectacle were treated to a visual, acoustic and emotional over-the-top mega-rock type show combined with spectacular circus feats. Eighteen dancers, 11 musicians, 8 acrobats, 6 singers and 2 actors performed breathtaking pieces choreographed to multi-media projections. The main actor, Karl Baumann rode over, then under and even inside a giant balloon as he carried the attentive crowd through his colorful yet busy dream (thus the delirium).

The theatrical production was so elaborate it required 20 truckloads (18 wheelers) of equipment. Some of this included: a 130-foot two-sided stage, 540 feet of projection screens (the equivalent of 4 IMAX's), an 80-foot volcano dress, 5 luminous swings and a multipurpose planet drum that also served as an acrobatic platform.

The "Delirium" show which deviated from the usual tent set-up of Cirque Du Soleil turned out to be one of the top grossing tours of Summer 2006.

Did you know Delirium was the first Cirque du Soleil show to use lyrics?

289) September 30

I'm not feeling blue anymore!

The Blue Man Group concert "How to Be a Megastar 2.0" (like Cirque du Soleil's "Delirium") shook the senses of the Mellon Arena patrons. As the title suggested the show was a rock concert and a spoof rock concert all at once. The 3 silent blue-painted performers played rhythmic avant-garde music and taunted audience members to get involved. One of the highlights of the multimedia spectacle was "Rock Concert Movements." Here a voice and a words-on-a-screen instructed fans to mimic typical concert actions-yet to do them in unison. At one point one had to imagine being lost in a maze of office cubicles and sewer pipes.

Did you know Blue Man Group once appeared on the finale of America's Got Talent? They performed a cover of the Who's Baba O'Riley with Tracy Bonham, from their Complex Rock Tour show. Bonham also played in Pittsburgh with "Blue Man Group."

290) October 21

This Penguin wasn't Staal-ing at all!

Were you there when the Pittsburgh Penguins defeated the Columbus Blue Jackets 5-3? In the game Penguin forward Jordan Staal set 2 NHL records in one night! First, he became the youngest player in league history to score two shorthanded goals in one game and second, he became the youngest player to score on a penalty shot.

Did you know on February 10, 2007 at the Air Canada Centre in Toronto, Jordan Staal became the youngest player in NHL history to score three goals (hat-trick) in one game? He was 18 years and 153 days old.

2007

<u>291) January 5</u>

Robert Morris didn't have a fighting chance against the Irish

In the feature game of the Inaugural Pittsburgh College Hockey Showcase, the Notre Dame Fighting Irish (No. 2) defeated the Robert Morris University Colonials 6-2. The sparse crowd of 3,412 witnessed a hat-trick by Kevin Deeth while teammate Erik Condra had a goal and 4 assists. Penguin prospect David Brown made 17 saves for the Irish. In the preliminary game that day the Washington and Jefferson club team defeated the Robert Morris non-varsity team 7-6.

Did you know that Robert Morris University is the only NCAA division 1 hockey program in the Pittsburgh area? Did you also know in 2008, Notre Dame were the finalists in the NCAA division 1 Ice Hockey Championships? They lost the final game 4-1 to perennial power house Boston College.

<u>292) March 23</u>

Skyrockets sizzle while Xplosion fizzle

In their last regular home game of season one, the Pittsburgh Xplosion wilted in defeat. The Minot Skyrockets (from North Dakota) thumped the home team119-106.The Xplosion finished the long year with a dismal 10 wins-38 loss record and out of the play-off picture. Fans attending this final game, however, got a few pleasant diversions. The Xplosion organization offered up the following. First, in a preliminary basketball contest the Pittsburgh Steelers football team took on a group of Pittsburgh celebrities. The latter included: former heavyweight boxing champion Roy Jones Jr., Steelers legends Dwayne Woodruff and Franco Harris, former NBA players Armen "The Hammer" Gilliam and Mike Iuzzolino, members of the Pittsburgh Pirates front office and local media personalities. Secondly, (and probably most important to the male patrons) at halftime of each game, the semi-finals and finals of the Hottest Hooters Girl contest was held.

Did you know the Pittsburgh Steelers have had an off-season charity basketball team since the 1960's?

293) April 15

Penguins taste post-season action after long drought

After a 6-year absence from the playoffs the Penguins faced first-round opponents the Ottawa Senators. This was Game 3 and the first one at the Mellon Arena since May 19, 2001. With the series tied at a game apiece the capacity crowd was anxious to see their Pens beat the Sens. It started well for the home team as "Scary Gary" Roberts scored on Ray Emery for the first goal of the game. The Senators tied it late in the first period then scored 3 more unanswered goals (2 by Captain Daniel Alfredsson) in the second period to put things out of reach. Sidney Crosby scored one in the third period but it was too little too late. The Senators won 4-2 and spoiled the Pens playoff party.

The Ottawa Senators eventually eliminated Pittsburgh 4 games to 1. They later advanced to the Stanley Cup Finals before losing to the Anaheim Ducks in 5 games.

Did you know Sidney Crosby became the first player to score in their first three NHL post-season games since 2001?

294) September 9

This was like a re-Genesis!

Were you there when the Mellon Arena welcomed music group Genesis on their "Turn It On Again" reunion tour? For the veteran band this was their first North American swing since 1992! Long suffering fans of the trio were rewarded with a trip down memory lane. The scrappy but fearless Phil Collins adeptly belted out most of the crowd favorites like Land of Confusion, Ripples, I Know What I Like (In Your Closet), Invisible Touch, I Can't Dance and Carpet Crawlers just like the old days. Meanwhile Mike Rutherford and Tony Banks kept pace perfectly on the guitar and keyboard respectively. One of the highlights came when Collins and Chester Thompson teamed up for a double drum solo. The power and synchronicity of the performance, leading into Los Endos, brought an ovation from the appreciative crowd.

Besides the precise music the concert featured a second to none lighting and screen show. While performing in outdoor stadiums on their "Turn It On Again" reunion tour, Genesis used the largest screen ever in concert history. It measured 210 feet wide by 40 feet high.

Two days after the Pittsburgh concert Genesis released their Turn It On Again (Tour Edition) double CD. The 34-hit collection included songs from as early as 1970. One of the highlights was the 1999 re-mix of the 1974's "The Carpet Crawlers" featuring Both Phil Collins and Peter Gabriel on lead vocals.

Did you know Genesis has sold more than 130 million records throughout its career?

295) September 14-15

"What so proudly we hail…"

For two days the show "Spirit of America" gave audience members a patriotic glimpse into the lives of those who help protect our freedoms. More than 300 soldiers from the U.S. Army Military District of Washington performed re-en-actments, drills and music to celebrate the 232-year history of the American Soldier. The performers, including 2 horses from The 3rd U.S. Infantry Regiment (The Old Guard Fife and Drum Corps) and the U.S. Army Band, "Pershing's Own," represented the oldest active-duty infantry unit in the Army. The elaborate production, which included battle scenes and simulated gunfire, used 100 robotic lighting fixtures, two audio trucks, two scenery trucks, a projection truck and 14 computers which synchronized all the elements of the show. Overall, 30,000 people took advantage of the free admission to these performances.

Did you know a couple days before this production, 4 members from the United States Army Drill Team gave a small clinic at the Hunt Armory for some students from Seneca Valley School District and Albert Gallatin High School?

296) November 9

Isn't he "Wonder-ful?"

It was a long time coming but Stevie Wonder made it back to the Mellon Arena. In fact the last show he performed in the building was July 22, 1972 as the opening act for the Rolling Stones. However on this night he was definitely the "main" act.

The concert began on a rather somber note as Stevie was led on stage by his daughter Aisha. Both were dressed in black from top to bottom. Stevie started the evening telling audience members of how his late mom came to him in a dream to tell him to get his (behind) out there on stage. By the way, his mother, Lula Mae Hardaway died on May 31, 2006 at the age of 76. She was a co-songwriter and helped Stevie write a number of his early hits including:

"Signed, Sealed, Delivered I'm Yours" and "I Was Made to Love Her." Stevie and his daughter then sang "Love is in Need of Love Today" with the band accompanying them much later.

After the slow start Wonder kicked into gear and blasted out a plethora of hits like: "Living for the City," "Master Blaster," "Golden Lady" and "If You Really Love Me." His voice didn't miss a beat as it hit every range superbly. His work on the keyboards wasn't too shabby either.

As things warmed up Wonder paid tribute to local band the Skyliners. He performed their hit "Since I Don't Have You." If you recall, Stevie's first wife, Syreeta Wright was from Pittsburgh. They were married on July 14, 1970 but were divorced a year and a half later.

Wonder kept the energy high and during his song Ribbon in the Sky had the audience split in two with the guys and gals singing in two-part harmony. By mid concert things picked up another notch as Wonder did a vocal and harmonica solo on "For Once in My Life." Then Stevie was on his knees for "I Was Made to Love Her" and stood on his piano for "Do I Do." The climax came with "Superstition" as Wonder belted out the lyrics to the 35-year old song with urgency and vigor.

Did you know Stevie Wonder has won 22 Grammy Awards? This is the most ever for a male solo artist.

2008

<u>297) January 4</u>

Montana mayhem

This Hannah Montana/Miley Cyrus concert with special guests the Jonas Brothers attracted a lot of undue attention. In this much anticipated show, Pittsburgh fans on September 29, 2007 bought every ticket within minutes of going on sale. Many people were left bitterly disappointed when they couldn't see their television idol live. Certain factors may have led to this unfortunate situation. One, there was only 11,000 tickets available to begin with. This was due to the stage layout and production specifications. Second, half of these tickets were reserved for the exclusive MileyWorld.com Fan Club members. Sadly many Pittsburgh Fan Club members were not able to secure pre-sale tickets due to the high demand. Third, some web sites (but not Ticket Master) were able to access and buy huge amounts of tickets at regular price and sell them for astronomical prices. For example, the highest priced ticket for the concert was $63.00 yet some on-line sites were asking $2,500.

Some of the fan club members who thought the ticket distribution process was unfair sought legal action. They hired Pittsburgh lawyer Rob Pierce who filed a class action lawsuit. Speaking on behave of his clients he stated "The $30.00 a year they paid to join this fan club really didn't do any good and we're trying to get that money back for those consumers." Meanwhile other fans took a more humorous approach in dealing with their predicament. For example, on January 4-the day of the concert, 8 dads at the Robinson Mall in Pittsburgh dressed up; wearing blonde wigs just like Hannah Montana and two-inch heals, for a "Drag Race". The event was sponsored by a local radio station with the winner getting 2 tickets to the show.

As for the show itself, the audience of predominately pre-teen and teen girls seemed to have enjoyed themselves. The singing, music, firecrackers, fireworks and confetti all blended into a superb evening of entertainment. However a couple mothers at the show were quite shocked. They were taken aback when Hannah Montana gyrated to certain songs wearing a tightly knitted sweater.

298) March 7-9

Disney does it with (High School) class!

Were you there when Disney's "High School Musical-The Ice Tour" glided into the Mellon Arena for three days? Pittsburgh audiences celebrated the sounds, songs, bop and pop of this phenomenal show that featured an awesome cast of 2 dozen world class skaters. Each performer brought high energy and skillful moves to the ice as they portrayed the roles of East High's own, Troy, Gabriella, Ryan, Sharpay, and Taylor. Fans heard chart-topping tunes like: "We're All in This Together," "Get'cha Head in the Game," "Start of Something New," "Stick to the Status Quo," and new music from "High School Musical 2." They were also mesmerized by the signature choreography made popular in the Emmy Award-winning Disney Channel Original Movie. On these nights the cool Igloo was literally transformed into a hot dance floor extraordinaire!

The main ice dancers in the show came with some impressive backgrounds. Amanda Billings (who portrayed Gabriella) for example, once competed in both the Canadian National and World Junior Figure Skating Championships. Fellow Canadian Adam Loosley (playing Ryan) was an All Ontario Champion and silver medalist in the 2000 Ontario Winter Games. Meanwhile Kristen Treni (in the role of Sharpay) from Jamestown, N.Y. was a 5-time U.S. National Championship competitor and the winner of the reality television show "Skating's Next Star."

Did you know "High School Musical-The Ice Tour" was performed in Spanish only in selected cities?

299) March 13-14

This preacher can pack them in

On these 2 evenings, Joel Osteen offered the faithful "A Night of Hope." The pastor of America's largest church (45,000 members) came to the Steel City to spread the good news. The famed televangelist and successful writer from Houston, Texas uplifted the attentive Mellon Arena audience with inspirational gospel messages, stories of hope and humorous side jokes. Osteen's wife Victoria, now a writer herself also addressed the faithful while Cindy Cruse Ratcliff and the Lakewood Band ensemble treated guests to electrifying music.

Many folks had a great vantage point to the stage as their seats were situated on the covered ice surface of the Mellon Arena. Most people enjoyed the close view and the positive messages Osteen extolled upon them. For a small minority however, the collection basket passed around was a bit much considering they paid money to be there in the first place.

Did you know the day after his "Night of Hope" Joel Osteen and his family met Senator Hillary Clinton at the Pittsburgh Omni William Penn Hotel? Senator Clinton was in town to pick up the endorsements (for the democratic presidential nominee) of the Mayor Luke Ravenstahl and County Executive Dan Onorato. Those endorsements were hand-delivered by Govenor Ed Rendell who was in town the night before. On the same morning (March 15) Senator Clinton and the above trio led the marching in the St. Patrick's Day Parade in Pittsburgh. Where did the parade route start? Of course the Mellon Arena!

300) March 27

She's Out of My (National Hockey) League

On this night the Pittsburgh Penguins welcomed back their chosen son Sidney Crosby. Crosby had been out of action since January 18 when he sustained a high ankle strain in the first period of a game against the Tampa Bay Lightning. Sid did return to play a few games in March but he was never 100 percent. His permanent return to the line-up this night helped the Pens beat the New York Islanders 3-1. In the same game ironically, newly acquired forward Marian Hossa got injured again. Hossa who was obtained from

Atlanta at the trading deadline initially hurt his knee while debuting for Pittsburgh on February 28.

While certain players on the ice made their return or exit, high above in the seating section there was some action also. During one sequence of the game an unruly fan was promptly escorted out of the Mellon Arena. Some fans looked concerned while others knew exactly what was going on. The scene, part of the movie "She's Out of My League" was being filmed during the live hockey game. The romantic comedy flick, shot in Pittsburgh, was about a man's lack of confidence that picks away at a relationship with the perfect woman. The film starred Alice Eve, Jay Baruchel and Krysten Ritter and was co-directed by Pittsburgh native Jim Miller.

Did you know Jim Miller is the brother of comedian and former Saturday Night Live star Dennis Miller?

301) May 24

Jumbo disappointment

Over 13,500 rabid Pittsburgh Penguin fans gathered at the Mellon Arena to watch the first game of the Stanley Cup Finals against the Detroit Red Wings. It was 16 years since the Penguins last won hockey's Holy Grail for the city of Pittsburgh. The atmosphere in the building was electric, the pre-game lighting show was awesome and the food was fantastic-the only thing missing were the players! That's because the game was actually being played in Detroit! Meanwhile back in Pittsburgh, Penguin officials showed the game on the Mellon Arena Jumbotron and fans cheered on the "home team" all night. However, it was a tough outing for the young Pens as Detroit blanketed them constantly. When all was said and done, the crowd left exhausted and disappointed as the Red Wings took the opener 4 to 0.

Did you know Detroit scored both a power play and short-handed goal in this game?

302) June 4

Penguins wish they had Wings

On this night the Detroit Red Wings narrowly defeated the Pittsburgh Penguins to capture the Stanley Cup. It was Game 6 of the series and Pittsburgh, having won game 5 in a dramatic triple overtime affair in Detroit kept things interesting to the very end. The Red Wings led 3-1 late in the third period. Then the Penguins were awarded a powerplay and the dramatic finish started. With Pens goalie Fleury on the bench for an extra attacker and the team with a two-man advantage Sergei Gonchar blasted a shot past Osgood. The crowd erupted as the score was now only 3-2. The game clock, now down to 87 seconds, had fans anxious for the ending. As play resumed Detroit kept the puck out of their end of the rink for a good chunk of time. However, as the last 8 seconds ticked away, the Penguins made a final surge. They gained the Red Wing blue line and Crosby fired a last attempt backhand shot. Osgood stopped the puck but didn't corral it. Hossa tried to poke in the rebound but couldn't get good wood on it. The final buzzer sounded and that was all she wrote. Detroit won their first Cup since 2002.

Henrik Zetterberg of the Detroit Red Wings won the Conn Smythe Trophy as the Most Valuable Player in the post-season while teammate Nicklas Lidstrom became the first European-born player to captain his team to a Stanley Cup Championship. Also, this was the only time in Mellon Arena history that the Stanley Cup was presented. The Penguins 2 Cup victories in the early 1990's were won in Minnesota and Chicago.

Did you know the Detroit Red Wings hold the distinction of having won more NHL titles (11) than any other U.S. team?

303) October 4

Would you like some Swedish meatballs with that Mellon?

In the 2008-09 home opener the Pittsburgh Penguins squeaked out a 4-3 victory when Tyler Kennedy scored in overtime. The Penguins, 2008 league finalists, faced the Ottawa Senators-in Sweden! Yes the game was played overseas at the sold-out Globe Arena in Stockholm but was shown on the Mellon Arena Jumbotron. During the game fans at the Igloo had the option to sit and watch the game, skate on the ice surface or take a tour of the arena. The attendance that day was probably a dismal 300. The Pens and Sens actually played each other twice in Sweden. On October 5 Ottawa gained a split by beating Pittsburgh 3-1.

Did you know this was the second time in franchise history the Penguins opened the season overseas? The first occurred in 2001 when they split a two-game series with the Nashville Predators in Tokyo, Japan.

304) October 27

Foreshadowing the future?

Presidential nominee Senator Barack Obama addressed 15,000 of the party faithful at the Mellon Arena this day. The Democratic rally started with Pennsylvania Senator Bob Casey and Governor Ed Rendell warming up the crowd. Once Senator Obama got to the stage Pittsburgh Steelers owner Dan Rooney presented him with a black and gold jersey. The crowd, seeing this exchange, broke out in unison singing "Here we go Steelers, Here we go." As the senator from Illinois lifted the jersey to his chest, it read "Obama 08". This signified the number of days until the election and the year of the election, 2008. Obama then gave a 35-minute address as part of the "closing argument" for his presidential campaign. As they say the rest is history. On November 4th Senator Obama became president-elect and on January 20, 2009 at the inauguration he was sworn in as the 44th President of the United States.

Did you know what song was playing in the background before Senator Obama took the stage at the Mellon Arena? It was Ain't No Stopping Us Now.

305) December 3-7

Please don't disturb these guys, they look a little hungry

On this night "Walking with Dinosaurs-The Live Experience" made big footprints in the hill district. Audiences at the Mellon Arena saw how the biggest and meanest creatures ever, ruled the earth! In all fifteen life-like and life-size dinosaurs walked, roared and fought for survival and supremacy. The biggest of these, the 75-foot Brachiosaurus and the ferocious Tyrannosaurus Rex with teeth up to 8 inches were highlights of this Broadway style theatrical spectacle. Engineers using technologies and techniques from film, animatronics, puppetry and physical theater gave fans young and old alike a "real" dinosaur experience.

Did you know a writer for the New York Times in describing the show said that dinosaurs are making "a thundering comeback after 65 million years?"

2009

306) January 7

You Shook Me All Night Long

Were you there when the bad boys from down under AC/DC rocked the joint? The concert which sold out in 18 minutes was part of the "Black Ice World Tour". After 35 years in the business AC/DC still delivered the goods as hard and loud as ever. Angus Young dressed in his signature schoolboy uniform pranced around and played guitar like a maniac. Meanwhile, lead singer Brian Johnson over 60 years old, belted out hit after hit in his rough but controlled raspy voice. Not missing a step in the fashion department Johnson donned his wardrobe piece, the cap. Overall, whether new or old fans, everyone got their fill tonight.

Did you know the 18-month "Black Ice World Tour" started on October 28, 2008 in Wilkes-Barre, Pennsylvania?

307) March 1

I've heard Rumors for many years

Fleetwood Mac made the Mellon Arena their "opening show" on their first tour in 5 years. Fans of the veteran group were hooked from the beginning and left the concert wanting even more. The "Unleashed" tour proved that the band whose average member was 60 years old could still play like they were 30. Prove of this came early and often as Stevie Nicks ripped through song after song with no hesitancy at all. The guys, no slouches themselves, kept an energetic tempo. Lindsey Buckingham played the guitar like it was part of his body while Mick Fleetwood banged on the drums like a possessed monkey. From the opening song Monday Morning to the final encore Silver Springs the band didn't miss a beat all night.

If you were at this concert you may recall who was absent from the band. Christie McVie a band member since 1970 retired in 1998.

Did you know Fleetwood Macs' song "Don't Stop" which was included in the concert lineup was also the theme song of the 1996 Clinton-Gore campaign?

308) March 27

Pop star creates a "Circus" while some crew members create a scene

After a five-year absence from the music scene Britney Spears came back with a vengeance. Sporting a new platinum-selling album (Circus), a new body and an elaborate stage show and choreography, Spears wowed the hungry Mellon Arena crowd. Fans yelled at the top of their voices "Brit-ney! Brit-ney!" long before Spears entered the circus stage and continued well after she left it. The comeback star didn't disappoint in singing her new songs (i.e. Womanizer etc.) along with her older hits (i.e. Oops I Did It Again etc.). The opening act for the sold out concert was the Pussycat Dolls.

Did you know 2 days before Britney performed at the Mellon Arena two of her road crew members, Alex Montes and Rockey Dickey got arrested by the Pittsburgh police? Apparently both men were on East Carson Street when a ruckus started. Reports say Dickey punched a guy in the face which was witnessed by a police officer. When the cop tried to break things up he got walloped by Dickey also. As a second officer emerged on the scene, Montes jumped him and put him into a headlock. Finally the policemen subdued Dickey when they tasered him. Meanwhile Montes fled the scene. He was later caught and the two rowdy roadies were arrested and charged with criminal conspiracy, disorderly conduct and public drunkenness.

309) June 9

The Stanley Cup arrives at the Mellon Arena but...

Hockey's Holy Grail, the Stanley Cup could have been presented tonight to the Detroit Red Wings for the second consecutive year. Rewind to a year ago and the scenario was the same. It was Game 6 of the Stanley Cup Finals and the Red Wings were leading the series 3 games to 2. Eventually they beat the Penguins 3-2 in a dramatic game to win their first Cup in 6 years. Pittsburgh, recalling that tough home loss, didn't want a repeat. This time they reversed their fortunes and edged the Red Wings 2 to 1. The game was a hard fought battle until the end. Jordan Staal and Tyler Kennedy had scored goals earlier off their own rebounds but it was the Pittsburgh defense that stole the show. Fleury made 25 great saves but none bigger than the breakaway by Dan Cleary with less than 2 minutes left in the third. Later with less than 15 seconds to play defenseman Rob Scuderi made 2 game-saving blocks while on his knees in the goal crease. Later when asked about his heroics he stated jokingly "I'm more of a stand-up goalie, not a butterfly."

As we all know by now Pittsburgh went into Detroit 2 days later and beat the Red Wings in Game 7. Max Talbot was the hero as he scored the Penguins only 2 goals in another 2-1 game. The victory, revenge from the year before, gave the Pens their third Stanley Cup in franchise history. All of them, ironically, were won on the road. After the game Evgeni "Geno" Malkin received the Conn Smythe trophy as the MVP in the playoffs while Crosby received the Stanley Cup as Captain of the Penguins.

Did you know in game 6 of the Stanley Cup Finals the Pittsburgh Penguins had a total of 20 blocked shots?

310) July 25

Brothers adds "Sparks" to their show

Were you their when the Jonas Brothers rode their popularity wave into the Steel City? Fresh off their release of their fourth album, Lines, Vines and Trying Times the boys didn't disappoint their mostly teenage girl audience. To warm up the sold-out Mellon crowd, former "American Idol" participant Jordin Sparks and new band Honor Society got things going. After their performances, the popular young brothers from New Jersey cranked things up in more ways than one. Nick, Joe and Kevin first appeared on a 140-foot stage-in-the-round with 2 added wing spaces then threw in a circular water screen, laser effects, motion automated videos, a giant crane which levitated over the audience, multiple risers, a trampoline and water guns. All of this added to the fun-filled entertaining atmosphere which even the moms in the audience enjoyed.

What distinguished the Jonas Brothers from most other boy bands was the fact that they actually played instruments. Some of the feature songs this night were: Paranoid, Poison Ivy, Hold On, Neil Diamond's Sweet Caroline, Gotta Find You, Live to Party and Lovebug. While on the piano Nick did a good solo job with A Little Bit Longer and Black Keys. He also took a moment to speak to the captive crowd about fighting diabetes. Being diabetic himself he encouraged his fans to educate and empower themselves about the condition.

Did you know the Jonas Brothers were the youngest band to make the cover of the Rolling Stone Magazine? They appeared on the July 2008 issue.

311) November 29

May the force be with you!

On this night the Mellon Arena was invaded by "Star Wars: In Concert." The multimedia event featured a live orchestra and choir performing music from all six scores by John Williams while massive movie screens showed footage of all the Star War movies. Narrating the whole show was actor Anthony Daniels who actually played C-3PO. Fans coming out to Mellon Arena also saw an exhibit of Star War paraphernalia which included: costumes, props, production artwork and other items.

Did you know on October 3, the first day tickets went on sale for "Star Wars: In Concert" the Mellon Arena held a special pre-event show? Fans were encouraged to dress up as their favorite Star Wars character while watching a two-hour "preview" on a large video screen outside Gate 3 of the Mellon Arena.

312) December 2

City game "site" takes a final bow

This night marked the last basketball game played between Pittsburgh and Duquesne at the Mellon Arena and it didn't disappoint. In fact Pittsburgh coach Jamie Dixon said: "This one will go down in history as probably the best (game here)…" What made the game (televised on CBS College Sports) so memorable was Pittsburgh's comeback-only their greatest in school history.

Pittsburgh never led the contest and by halftime they were down 33-20. Later the deficit rose to 16 points as Duquesne appeared to be poised for their first "City Game" victory after 8 consecutive defeats. With just 14 minutes left to play Pittsburgh sensing their demise switched to a zone defensive. The bold move paid off as Duquesne managed only 7 points the rest of the way. Pittsburgh meanwhile chipped away at the huge lead. Then with just over 2 minutes to go, Pittsburgh guard Ashton Gibbs tied the score at 53 with a nifty 3-pointer. Later, as the clock ticked away, both teams had numerous opportunities to win. Neither converted and when the final buzzer sounded the game was deadlocked. In the first overtime, defensive ruled once again. However this time Duquesne got into the act also. They limited the Panthers to just 3 points but unfortunately scored only 3 themselves. In double overtime, Gibbs led Pittsburgh with a pair of 3-pointers as the Panthers took their first significant lead. They held on dearly the rest of the way for a dramatic 67-58 victory. What a fitting end to a long-standing Mellon Arena rivalry!

Did you know Pittsburgh guard Ashton Gibbs was only 1 for 12 in regulation play?

313) December 21

Brodeur breaks NHL record

On this night veteran goalie Martin Brodeur of the New Jersey Devils made NHL history when he recorded his 104th regular season career shutout. The previous record of 103 was held by Hall of Fame goalie Terry Sawchuk. Ironically both goalies got their record shutouts against the Pittsburgh Penguins.

In the game Brodeur stopped all 35 shots as his Devils blanked the Pittsburgh Penguins 4-0. After the record breaking effort, teammates congratulated him while the remaining Pens fans applauded him. In addition, a congratulatory message from Penguins owner Mario Lemieux was read on the public address system. Just two games earlier, Brodeur set another NHL record when he appeared in his 1,030 game-the most ever by a goalie.

Did you know on March 17, 2009 Martin Brodeur broke another NHL record? When the New Jersey Devils beat the Chicago Blackhawks 3-2, Brodeur collected win number 552. The previous record was held by Patrick Roy at 551.

2010

314) April 8

The last "regular season" puck drop

On this night the Pittsburgh Penguins played their final ever regular season game at the Mellon Arena. For those into statistics it was home game number 1,667 in franchise history. The first one, played on October 11, 1967 saw the Montreal Canadiens defeat the Penguins 2-1.

Before the puck drop the hockey team honored 50 former Penguins in a classy red-carpet ceremony. Among those in attendance were: Jack Riley (first general manager of the Penguins), Red Sullivan (first coach of the Penguins), 77 year-old Andy Bathgate (scored first goal in franchise history), Les Binkley (first starting goalie of the Penguins), Kent Schinkel, Gene Ubriaco, Ed Olczyk and Rick Kehoe (the only men who have coached and played for the team), Eddie Johnston (general manager who drafted Mario Lemieux in 1984 and the winningest coach in franchise history with 232 wins), Jean Pronovost, (first Penguin to score 50 goals) and his line mates Syl Apps and Lowell MacDonald (all part of the Century Line), Pierre Larouche (the first player to score 50 goals in a season for 2 different teams), Greg Malone (former head scout and father of current Tampa Bay Lightning player Ryan Malone), Mark Johnson (Gold medal winner in 1980 at Lake Placid and son of legendary coach Bob Johnson), Phil Bourque and Bob Errey (current radio and television color commentators for the Penguins), Brian Trottier (6-time Stanley Cup winner), Craig Patrick (17-year general manager of the Penguins), Paul Coffey and Larry Murphy (hall of fame defensemen) and Mario Lemieux (all-time Penguin leading scorer, 2-time Stanley Cup winner and owner of the Penguins). All these, along with the rest of the alumni had a group photo taken with the current Pittsburgh Penguin players.

As for the game this night, the Penguins destroyed the New York Islanders 7-3. Sidney Crosby scored his 49th goal and what appeared to be his 50th. However, later review showed it was deflected by Bill Guerin. Crosby did receive an assist on the play which counted for his 500th career point, making him the third youngest player to reach that mark. Only Wayne Gretzky and Mario Lemieux got there faster. As for Guerin's deflected goal, his 20th of the year, it put him into the NHL record books. He became the first NHL player to have scored 20 or more goals a season for 7 different teams. Guerin's other 20-goal teams were the: New Jersey Devils, Edmonton Oilers, Boston Bruins, Dallas Stars, St. Louis Blues and the New York Islanders.

After the game the festive atmosphere continued as Penguins players gave away their signed shirts as part of Fan Appreciation Night.

315) May 12

Blame Canada!

In a quest to capture their second Stanley Cup in a row, the Pittsburgh Penguins were unceremoniously dumped by the Montreal Canadiens 5-2 in Game 7 of the Eastern Conference Semifinals of the 2010 NHL Playoffs. With the defeat, the Pens would end their season and play their final game ever at the historical Mellon Arena. Ironically the Canadiens handed the Penguins their first ever franchise loss (see entry 314 above) and would do the same tonight.

In this Game 7 the Canadiens tallied a power play goal just 32 seconds into the first frame and then added 3 more unanswered ones to build a commanding 4-0 lead. Current Montreal captain Brian Gionta had a goal while Penguin-killer Mike Cammalleri added his 7th of the series. The Penguins got goals from Chris Kunitz and Jordan Staal to cut the lead in half but it wasn't enough. The Habs continued their stifling defensive play while upstart Slovakian-born goalie Jaroslav Halak stopped the rubber the rest of the way. With 10 minutes left to play Gionta scored his second goal (and 7th of the playoffs) that put the final nail in the Pens coffin.

Did you know after this game many Pittsburgh fans stayed to watch a video montage to the nation's first and only retractable roof indoor arena? Meanwhile back in Montreal 21,000 Canadiens fans filed out of the Bell Centre (where they had watched the game on video) and joined others on the street to celebrate the improbable victory. Things got a little rowdy and by the end of the night Montreal Police had arrested 25 people.

316) June 26

Will You (Still) Love Me Tomorrow

As a final farewell to the grand daddy of all arenas musical icons James Taylor and Carole King teamed up to play a concert from their Troubadour Reunion Tour. It was February 26, 1971 since they last performed here together. This time around a more intimate setting was in order. For example, some of the seats were set up as "stage seating" with tables for two surrounding the stage. Folks willing to pay for these special seats helped benefit local and national charities including Natural Resources Defense Council and the Alliance for the Wild Rockies.

The close proximity to the performers enhanced their musical appreciation. Moreover, it even prompted one fan to yell out "You're still damn cute, Carole!" Many would have agreed considering the 68 year-old King looked better than many women half her age. The blonde curls and contagious smile didn't hurt either.

Throughout the evening Taylor and King "wowed" the crowd with hit after hit. At one point Taylor played "Carolina in My Mind," "Sweet Baby James" and "The Secret of Life" on a moving carousel. The songs moved him physically but moved the audience emotionally. Ironically, this set of tunes got musical help from Danny Kortchmar, Russ Kunkel and Leland Sklar-the same three who played with him at the 1971 Civic Arena concert! As for King songs like "So Far Away," "Smackwater Jack," "A Natural Woman," "I Feel the Earth

Move," and "It's Too Late" sparked memories but it was her rendition of "Will You Still Love Me Tomorrow" that garnered a standing ovation.

Taylor, his voice still clear and sharp had the crowd clapping in appreciation with "Mexico", "Shower the People" and "You've Got a Friend" but had them on their feet with the completion of "Fire and Rain".

In this fitting and historical night Taylor and King performed 28 memorable songs. The encore included: "Up on the Roof", maybe a tribute to the once retractable roof above them, "How Sweet It Is" and "You Can Close Your Eyes"-the final song ever performed at the Civic/Mellon Arena.

Did you know James Taylor's first #1 hit in 1971 was "You've Got a Friend"? The song, written by Carole King, appears on her famous Tapestry album of the same year.

2006

286. http://music.musictnt.com/biography/sdmc_Civic_Arena

287. http://www.nhl.com/news/2006/04/269074.html

288. http://www.post-gazette.com/pg/06180/701905-42.stm

289. Pittsburgh Post-Gazette, October 3, 2006, page number C-3

289. http://theurbangorilla.blogspot.com/2007/01/blue-man-group-concert.html

290. http://enwikipedia.org/wiki/Jordan_Staal

2007

291. Pittsburgh Post-Gazette, January 6, 2007 page number F-8

291. http://en.wikipedia.org/wiki/Frozen_Four

292. Pittsburgh Post Gazette, March 24, 2007

293. http://www.post-gazette.com/pg/07101/776784-61.stm

294. http://en.wikipedia.org/wiki/Mellon_Arena

294. http://www.rhino.com/rzine/pressrelease.lasso?PRID=513

295. www.mdw.army.mil/content/anmviewer.asp?a=1955&print=yes

295. www.mdw.army.mil/content/anmviewer.asp?a=1964&print=yes

296. kdka.com/local/Stevie.Wonder.Pittsburgh.2.564544

2008

297. http://mellonarena.com/site.php?pageID=4&eID=21

297. http://kdka.com/local/Hannah.Montana.concert.2.623143.html

297. http://www.thepittsburghchannel.com/news/14307986/detail.html

298. http://www.pittsburghlive.com/x/event/?com=detail&eID=22540

298. http://en.wikipedia.org/wiki/Amanda_Billings

299. Pittsburgh Post-Gazette, March 10, 2008

299. http://www.pittsburghlive.com/x/pittsburghtrib/blogs/primarycolors/index.php?archive=March%202008

300. Pittsburgh Post Gazette, March 28, 2008

301. Pittsburgh Post Gazette, May 25, 2008

302. Pittsburgh Post Gazette, June 5, 2008

303. Pittsburgh Post Gazette, October 5, 2008

304. Pittsburgh Post Gazette, October 28, 2008

305. Pittsburgh Post Gazette, December 4, 2008

2009

306. Pittsburgh Post Gazette, January 8, 2009

307. Pittsburgh Post Gazette, March 2, 2009

308. perezhilton.com

308. Pittsburgh Post Gazette, March 26 & 27, 2009

309. Pittsburgh Post-Gazette, June 10 & June 13, 2009

310. Pittsburgh Post Gazette, July 26, 2009

311. Pittsburgh Post Gazette, October 1, 2009

312. Pittsburgh Post Gazette, December 3, 2009

313. Pittsburgh Post Gazette, December 22, 2009

313. USA Today, December 22, 2009

2010

314. Pittsburgh Post Gazette, April 9, 2010

315. The Associated Press, thecanadianpress.com Updated: May 13, 2010

316. Pittsburgh Post Gazette.com, June 27, 2010

Conclusion

I hope you have enjoyed this trip down memory lane. For me it has been a labor of love highlighting many of the special moments of the Pittsburgh Civic/Mellon Arena. When I first started researching events held at the "Igloo" I had no idea how many (over 7,000) or how diverse they were (roller hockey to religious). Whether big or small, amateur or professional they have all touched the lives of people in Pittsburgh. In reading this book you probably said at times "Yes, now I remember!" or "Wow what a game that was!" or even "That was the date of the Elvis concert!" Collectively we can cherish these great memories and feel a sense of pride. With the new arena (Consol Energy) hopefully a brand new set of memories will be created.